Living & Retiring in Spain

Living & Retiring In Spain

PHILIP BARKER

BLANDFORD

Since the entry of Spain into the European Economic Community there are on-going changes in many aspects of Spanish life, especially in the relation to the law as it applies to tax and immigration. This book has been written with the greatest care to ensure accuracy. But it must be remembered that it can be only an introduction to life and retirement in Spain and should not be regarded as a substitute for the essential professional advice that is readily available in Spain and in the UK.

Neither the author nor the publisher can assume responsibility for any action performed as a result of its perusal.

First published in the UK 1989 by Blandford Publishing,
an imprint of Cassell plc
Artillery House, Artillery Row, London SW1P 1RT

Copyright © 1989 Philip Barker-Benfield

Distributed in the United States by
Sterling Publishing Co., Inc.,
2 Park Avenue, New York, NY 10016

Distributed in Australia by
Capricorn Link (Australia) Pty Ltd,
PO Box 665, Lane Cove, NSW 2066

British Library Cataloguing in Publication Data
Barker, Philip
  Living and retiring in Spain.
  1. Overseas retirement. For British
  personnel
  I. Title
  646.7'9

ISBN 0-7137-2079-4

All rights reserved. No part of this book may be reproduced
or transmitted in any form or by any means, electronic or
mechanical, including photocopying, recording or any
information storage and retrieval system, without
permission in writing from the publisher.

This book is sold subject to the conditions that it shall not,
by way of trade or otherwise, be lent, re-sold, hired out
or otherwise circulated without the publisher's prior
consent in any form of binding or cover other than that
in which it is published and without a similar condition including
this condition being imposed on the subsequent purchaser.

Phototypeset by Input Typesetting Ltd, London SW19 8DR

Printed by Mackays of Chatham PLC, Chatham, Kent

Contents

1 An Introduction to Spain   1
2 Principal Retirement Areas   10
3 Visa Requirements   17
4 Investing in Property   19
5 Paying for Your Property   39
6 Banking in Spain   45
7 Public Services and Utilities   52
8 Taking up Residence   58
9 Living in Spain   68
10 Leisure Pursuits   74
11 Cultural Life   87
12 Leaving Your Spanish Home   94
13 Working in Spain   96
14 Hibernation Rather than Emigration   97

Glossary of Spanish Terms   98

Useful Addresses in the UK   101

Index   103

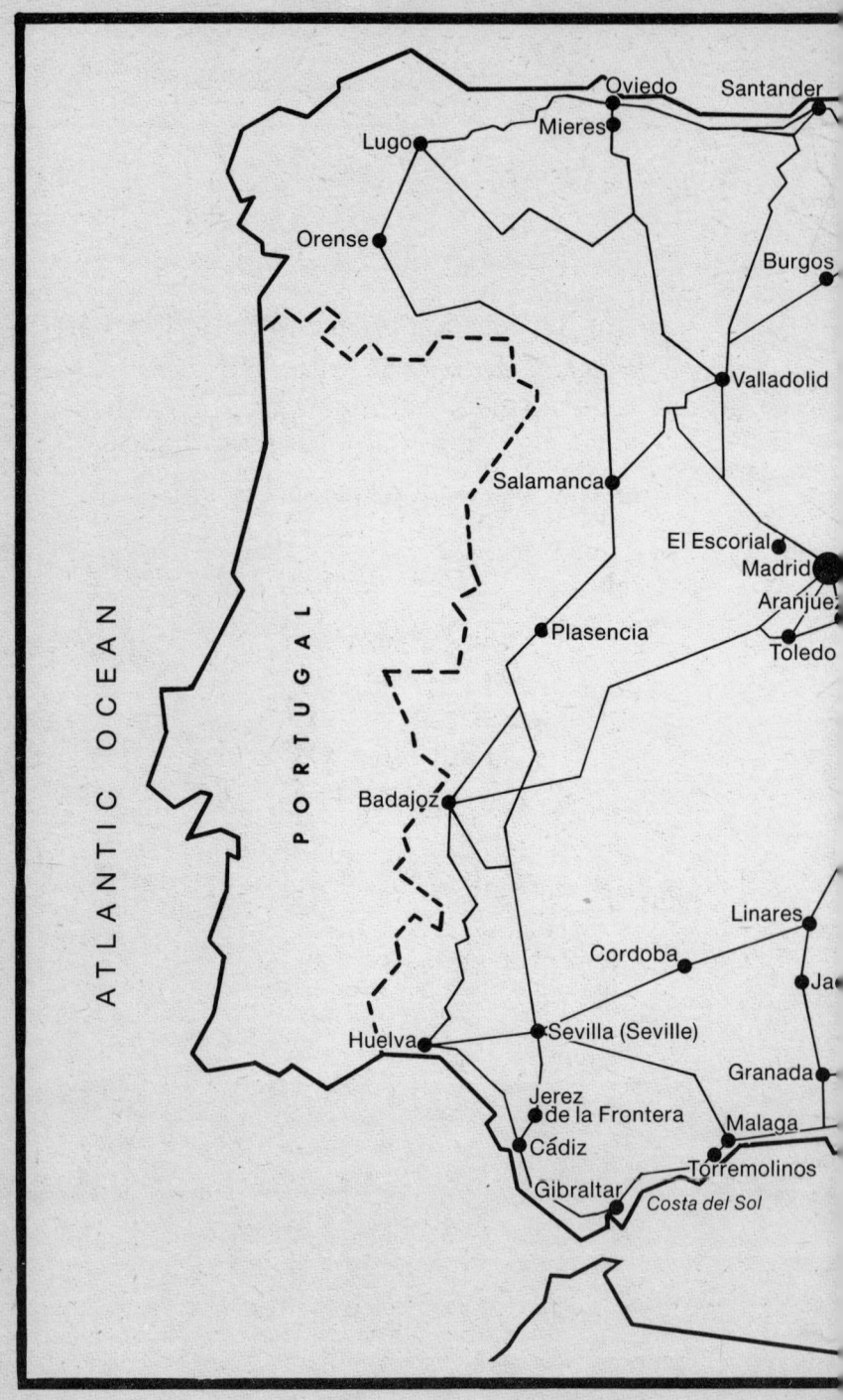

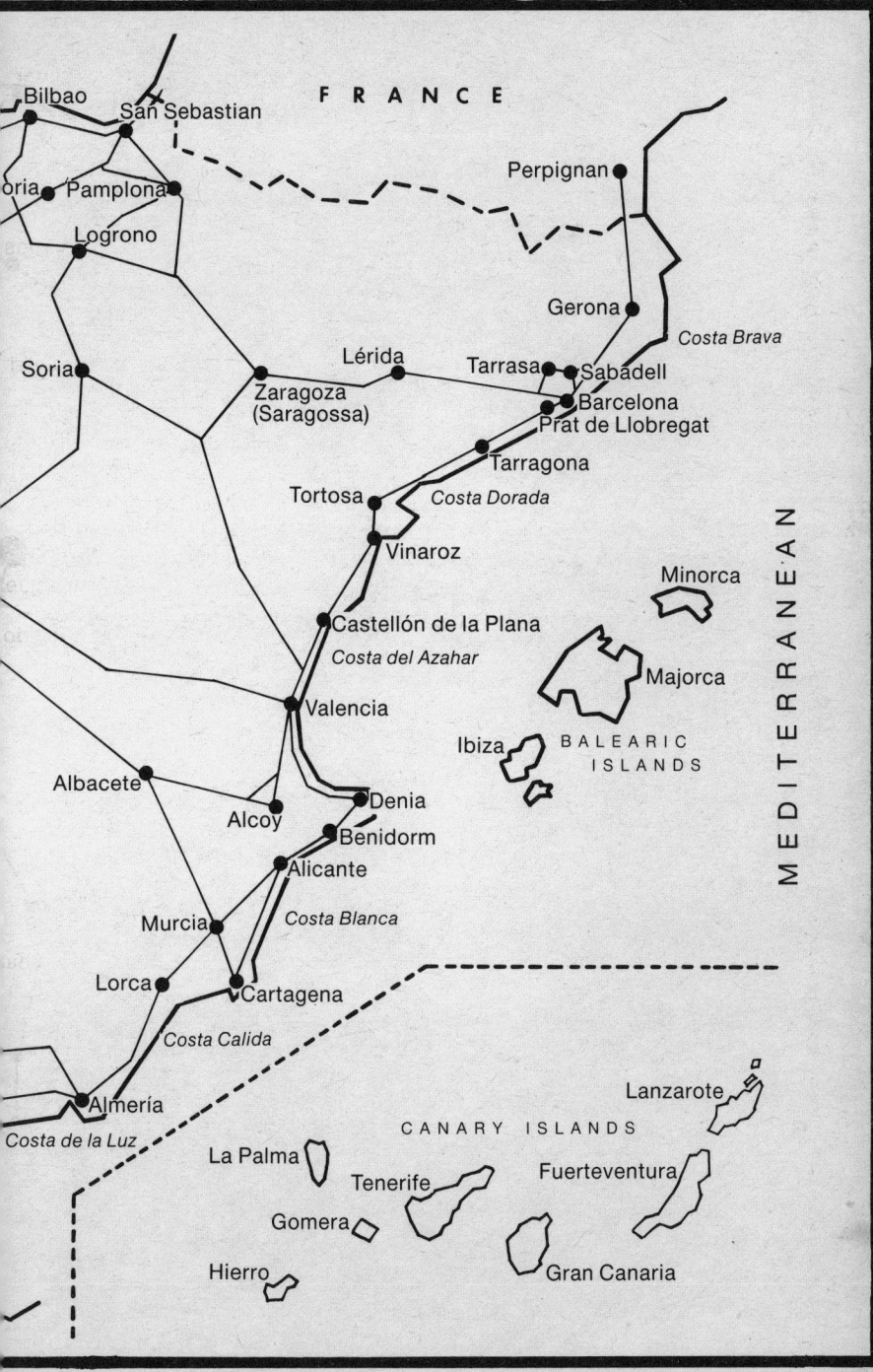

1
An Introduction to Spain

THE KINGDOM OF SPAIN

The Kingdom of Spain occupies eleven-thirteenths of the Iberian Peninsula. It is bounded by the Pyrenees separating it from France in the north, by Portugal in the west, by the Atlantic in the north and the south-west and the Mediterranean in the south and south-east. The Balearic Islands of Mallorca, Menorca, Ibiza, Formentera and Cabrera in the Mediterranean are approximately 150 miles east of Valencia. The seven islands of volcanic origin comprising the Canaries group in the Atlantic ocean off the west coast of Africa, form two Spanish provinces. The small enclaves of Ceuta and Melilla situated on the Mediterranean coast of Morocco are also administered as part of Spain.

With an area of 194,800 square miles, Spain is roughly twice the size of the UK, whose nearly fifty-six million inhabitants produce a population density of 590 per square mile. In Spain, the density is only one-third of that of the UK at 193 per square mile and, except in some of the industrial areas in the north and at the major tourist resorts in high season, this is immediately noticeable.

In addition to Spanish, the Basque, Catalan, Galician and other regional languages are spoken in their ethnic areas whilst a great number of Spaniards are fluent in English, especially in the capital and in the tourist areas.

Mainland Spain and the Balearic Islands are in the Greenwich Mean Time (GMT) plus 1 time zone (GMT plus 2 in summer) whilst the Canary Islands, although they are further west, keep Greenwich Mean Time, except in the period April to September when it is GMT plus 1.

The electricity supply, most of it from hydro-electric and

atomic generating stations, is 220 volts, 50 cycles almost everywhere. The metric system is used for weights and measures.

A GLIMPSE OF HISTORY

Originally settled by a tribe of dark, long-headed Iberians, Spain was successively occupied by Carthaginians, Celts, Romans, Vandals and Visigoths. By the fifth century AD it was Christian, but then in the eighth century Islamic Moors from North Africa invaded and the country remained under their domination until the fall of the Kingdom of Granada at the Christian re-conquest in the fifteenth century. Once again Christian, Spain became the defender of Roman Catholicism.

In 1492 Christopher Columbus, under the auspices of King Ferdinand V and his Queen Isabella, sailed from northern Spain to discover the New World. In the ensuing years Francisco Pizarro conquered Peru and Hernán Cortés Mexico. Thus was laid the foundation of the Spanish Empire which, at its zenith, comprised much of North, Central and South America, Cuba, Puerto Rico and some other Caribbean islands, the Netherlands and parts of Italy and Germany in Europe and the Philippine islands in the Far East.

Wars of independence in the Spanish colonies, commencing in South America, gradually reduced the size of the Spanish Empire until, by the end of the nineteenth century, Cuba and Puerto Rico and the Philippines were lost in a war with the United States of America.

The early twentieth century saw several political upheavals and the exile of King Alfonso XIII in 1931. Then, in 1936, the Popular Front government—a coalition of socialists, communists, republicans and anarchists—was challenged by the army under General Francisco Franco. A civil war followed with both sides receiving aid from abroad; Franco from Germany and Italy, and the Republicans from France, Russia and Mexico.

The civil war ended in 1939 and General Franco, who was named 'Caudillo' or leader, managed to maintain the neutrality of Spain during World War 2, which started the same year. He ruled Spain until his death in 1975, after which Juan Carlos I of Borbón y Borbón was sworn in as king and head of state. Free elections were held in June 1976 and today Spain is a constitutional monarchy with a democratically elected government, a member of the North Atlantic Treaty Organisation and of the European Economic Community.

SPAIN AS A RETIREMENT HAVEN

This book is written as a general introduction to residence in Spain, for those who, on retirement, are planning to live there permanently with a concomitant change of domicile.

Southern Spain is rapidly becoming one of the most favoured regions for those seeking a temporary or permanent retirement residence in a warm, equable climate, within the European Economic Community and fairly close to the UK. There is perhaps no place in Europe which offers as great a variety of properties at relatively reasonable prices or where life can be more easily tailored to one's needs and income, than the coastal and immediate hinterland area of this part of the Iberian Peninsula.

Spain offers an enormous amount of land and accommodation from which to choose: mountain, beach and riverside terrain, land wooded with pine, olive, almond, citrus and many other trees, studio flats, large luxury apartments, sophisticated penthouses, villas small and large, country estates, town and village houses, farmhouses for conversion, wind and water mills; all of these can be found in the portfolios of Spanish estate agents and developers and their representatives in Britain.

The most popular places, accessible by air, train or road from northern Europe, are in Catalonia, Valencia, Murcia and Andalusia, along the littoral stretching from the French border at Port Bou, past Gibraltar to Cádiz and Huelva to the Portuguese frontier. The areas attracting mass tourism are parts of the Costa Brava, the Costa Blanca, the Costa del Sol and some of the newly named sub-Costas at the edges of each. Between these strips of intense tourist development, and in the foothills of many of the mountain ranges behind them, are vast regions of truly rural Spain, increasingly attracting those who prefer the less claustrophobic life-style of country living but who wish to remain within easy reach of the facilities of the resorts or cities.

The Barcelona-Cádiz highway, the N340, links all the coastal regions and connects at irregular intervals with the minor roads that lead to the hinterland past farms and almond and olive groves, deep into vineyard-covered foothills and on to the mountains, often snow-capped in winter. They wind their way past hamlets and villages where in places life, except for the intrusion of the twentieth century in the form of the motor car and the television aerial, has changed little since the days of Cervantes and Don Quixote.

DOMICILE

A democracy since 1976, Spain became a member of the European Economic Community early in 1986. Thus it is, in some ways, similar to Britain in the mid-1970s after EEC entry: subject to changes, often frequent, in rules, regulations and procedures.

Domicile is perhaps the most important matter affecting all seekers of residence abroad and should be considered at an early stage. It is that legal relationship between a person and a territory, subject to a distinctive legal system, which allows the person to invoke the system as his or her personal law. Put more prosaically, if somewhat less accurately, it refers to the country to which a person 'belongs', the country which is his or her 'natural home'. There are several forms of domicile, but the one which would apply to persons who, on retirement, move permanently to Spain is the 'domicile of intent'.

In practical terms it would not be simple for you, as a person of UK origin who retired to Spain, to establish that you had become domiciled there. If a UK property is retained, the Inland Revenue will naturally conclude that you have not finally resolved to live the rest of your life abroad that you remain legally domiciled in the UK and thus are subject to British taxes. At the same time, if you spend 183 days in a year in Spain, you will be considered by the Spanish revenue to be subject to the tax system there. This problem may be largely resolved by the

An Introduction to Spain

1977 Double Taxation Agreement between the UK and Spain, providing you maintain no home in the UK and make all possible efforts to establish Spanish domicile as soon as possible. For a retired couple (since husband and wife are considered together for most tax purposes, but are taken separately for residence purposes) this can be done most visibly by:
1   Selling your home in the UK and any other property there.
2   Resigning from all clubs and associations in the UK.
3   Both of you moving to Spain as soon as a site for a residence has been located for you to buy or build. In the latter case you might lease a dwelling during the construction period, as you will probably wish to oversee the work and also you will be able to build up your residence time there.
4   Joining clubs in Spain.
5   Drawing up and registering a Spanish will according to Spanish law.
6   Planning to be buried in Spain. Most Spanish graves are 'wall niches' rented for periods, so you could arrange for the eventual return of your remains to a family grave in the UK, if you so wished.

There will be a time-lag between your taking up residence in Spain and the Inland Revenue recognising your 'domicile of intent'. With the aid of your lawyers and a Spanish *Asesor Fiscal* (financial consultant) and the Double Taxation Agreement, you can be steered through this intervening period with the minimum tax liability in each country. After this you may find that you will be paying less tax in Spain than you would pay were you still domiciled in the UK.

CLIMATE

The Mediterranean sea tempers the weather conditions of the Spanish southern littoral so that extremes of temperature are seldom encountered. Nevertheless, the cold north and north-easterly winds of winter which bring snow to the Pyrenees and the Sierra Nevada, and sometimes to the central plain, occasionally reach the coasts. The most preferable locations are those protected by mountain ranges. With few exceptions, most of the popular retirement areas are so insulated. Firestone Hispania, a multi-national tyre manufacturer, publishes a wide range of maps of Spain. Its 'touristic' series shows in relief the Sierra Bermeja, the Sierra Blanca, the Almijaras and the Alpujarras: the ranges which, together with the Sierra Nevada and the eastern Pyrenees, most influence the climate of the major resorts. The same mountains tend in summer to filter the hot winds from the central plain and the north and thus maintain comfortable temperatures throughout most of the year, hence the near perfection of climate. From these maps it is possible to judge the amount of protection afforded to each area.

Humidity and its effects, however, are important considerations. High humidity accentuates the sensation of temperature, both hot and cold, whilst low humidity has the opposite effect. Humidity increases the closer one is to the sea or any large body of water, but it varies according to wind velocity and direction.

Apart from comfort, maintenance costs of buildings vary in direct ratio to the percentage of humidity, especially near the sea, where the air also has a high saline content. In general, humidity in southern Spain is within the 'comfort zone' for most of the year.

GETTING TO SPAIN

The fastest way to Spain from the UK is, of course, by air, by charter or scheduled flights.

Charter flights

These are fractionally cheaper than scheduled flights, but most are a mixture of package-tourists and seat-only passengers at peak periods, and, as charter airlines must operate at full capacity to be viable, they are usually packed. Aeroplanes earn money only whilst actually in the air so a charter aircraft's utilisation hours are kept as high as possible and planes will make several long-distance flights each day. Thus, in the event of delays accumulating, passengers booked for certain charter services may have a long wait at the airport before take-off. When one takes into account the airport charges which some

Average temperatures as supplied by the Spanish meteorological Office (Fahrenheit and Centigrade)

TOWN AND AREA		Jan °F	Jan °C	Feb °F	Feb °C	Mar °F	Mar °C	Apr °F	Apr °C	May °F	May °C	June °F	June °C	Jul °F	Jul °C	Aug °F	Aug °C	Sept °F	Sept °C	Oct °F	Oct °C	Nov °F	Nov °C	Dec °F	Dec °C
Cape Bagur (Costa Brava)	Max	57	14	57	14	61	16	63	17	68	20	74	23	80	27	78	26	77	25	69	21	62	16	54	15
	Min	43	6	43	6	46	8	49	9	55	18	60	16	65	18	69	21	62	17	55	13	49	9	45	7
Barcelona (Costa Dorada)	Max	56	13	58	14	61	16	65	18	70	21	77	25	83	28	83	28	77	25	70	21	61	16	56	13
	Min	43	6	45	7	49	9	52	11	58	14	65	18	70	21	70	21	66	19	59	15	52	11	47	8
Valencia (Costa del Azahar)	Max	59	15	61	16	65	18	68	20	74	23	79	26	84	29	84	29	81	27	74	23	66	19	61	16
	Min	43	6	43	8	47	6	50	10	56	13	61	16	66	19	68	20	65	18	59	15	50	10	45	7
Alicante (Costa Blanca)	Max	61	16	63	17	68	20	72	22	78	26	84	29	90	32	90	32	86	30	77	25	70	21	63	17
	Min	44	7	43	6	47	8	50	10	56	13	61	15	66	19	68	20	65	18	59	15	50	10	45	7
Murcia (Costa Calida)	Max	59	15	61	16	65	18	67	19	74	23	77	25	84	29	84	29	81	27	75	24	68	20	63	17
	Min	41	5	41	5	47	8	49	9	56	13	63	17	68	20	68	20	65	18	58	14	50	10	45	7
Malaga (Costa del Sol)	Max	63	17	63	17	67	19	70	21	74	23	81	27	84	29	86	30	84	29	74	23	68	20	63	17
	Min	49	9	49	9	52	11	56	13	59	15	66	19	70	21	72	22	68	20	61	16	54	12	49	9

TOWN AND AREA		Jan °F	Jan °C	Feb °F	Feb °C	Mar °F	Mar °C	Apr °F	Apr °C	May °F	May °C	June °F	June °C	Jul °F	Jul °C	Aug °F	Aug °C	Sept °F	Sept °C	Oct °F	Oct °C	Nov °F	Nov °C	Dec °F	Dec °C
Cadiz (Costa de la Luz)	Max	59	15	58	14	65	18	70	21	74	23	81	27	84	29	86	30	84	29	74	23	68	20	63	17
	Min	47	8	45	7	52	11	54	12	59	15	65	18	68	20	68	20	66	19	59	15	54	12	49	9
Santander (Cornisa Cantabria)	Max	54	12	54	12	59	15	59	15	63	17	67	19	72	22	72	22	70	21	65	18	59	15	54	12
	Min	45	7	45	7	47	8	50	10	52	11	58	14	61	16	64	18	59	15	54	12	50	10	47	8
Pontevedra (Galicia)	Max	58	14	59	15	61	16	65	18	68	20	75	24	77	25	79	26	75	24	68	20	61	16	58	14
	Min	38	3	40	4	41	5	45	7	50	10	54	12	56	13	56	13	54	12	49	9	43	6	41	5
Madrid (Castilla)	Max	49	9	52	11	59	15	65	18	70	21	81	27	88	31	86	30	77	25	66	19	56	13	49	9
	Min	34	1	36	2	41	5	54	12	50	10	58	14	63	17	63	17	58	14	50	10	41	5	36	2
Sevilla (Inland Andalucia)	Max	59	15	63	17	69	21	74	23	79	26	90	32	95	35	97	36	90	32	79	26	68	20	61	16
	Min	43	6	43	6	49	9	52	11	56	13	63	17	69	21	68	20	65	18	58	14	50	10	45	7
Mallorca (Baleares)	Max	58	14	59	15	63	17	67	19	72	22	79	26	84	29	84	29	81	27	74	23	65	18	59	15
	Min	43	6	43	6	47	8	50	10	56	13	63	17	66	19	68	20	65	18	58	14	50	10	47	8
Las Palmas (Canarias, East)	Max	70	21	70	21	72	22	73	23	74	23	76	24	77	25	79	26	79	26	80	27	75	24	72	22
	Min	61	16	61	16	61	16	63	17	65	18	66	19	70	21	72	22	72	22	70	21	65	18	63	17
Tenerife (Canarias, West)	Max	68	20	70	21	72	22	74	23	76	24	79	26	83	28	84	29	83	28	79	26	75	24	70	21
	Min	58	14	58	14	59	15	61	16	63	17	66	19	68	20	70	21	70	21	66	19	63	17	61	16

(Table supplied courtesy of the Spanish Meteorological Office).

An Introduction to Spain

travel firms impose in addition to their advertised fare, and the cost of the often obligatory insurance against delays and cancellation, plus the risk of last-minute changes of flight times and even airports at peak periods, a scheduled flight from a principal airport can be well worth the additional cost, unless one is on a package tour. There are charter as well as scheduled flights to Spain from many British airports, with the exception of London Heathrow.

Scheduled flights
British Airways and Iberia offer daily flights from a number of UK airports throughout the year. The average flight time is two and one-half hours.

By train
Daily train services via a number of Channel crossings connect London, via Paris, with the Spanish Mediterranean provinces. Journey time can be up to 48 hours.

By road
Road distance between the UK and southern Spain varies according to Channel crossing, destination and trans-France route. London to Málaga is about 1500 miles via western France, the Hendaye-Irún frontier and Madrid. It is approximately 350 miles longer via Paris, Orange, Perpignan, La Jonquera and Barcelona. It is also possible to make this trip by coach.

By ship and road
A popular route is by car ferry from Portsmouth to Santander in northern Spain and thence by road via Madrid. This entails 24 hours at sea and then about 560 miles by road.

By air and bus
A relatively new route is by air or train to Madrid and from there a 7-hour journey in an air-conditioned bus to Málaga. Similar bus services connect Madrid with a number of other southern resorts and cities.

2
The Principal Retirement Areas

The many popular retirement areas of Spain are mostly located in, or within reasonable distance of, the best-known resorts along the southern coasts.

Of Spain's 1300 miles of coastline, the littoral of the Mediterranean and the Atlantic which stretches from Port Bou, at the French frontier, to the River Guadiana which marks the Portuguese border at Ayamonte, is divided into eight major coastal areas or 'Costas'.

The area of south and west Spain known as Andalusia (roughly translated as 'Towards the Sun') embraces the provinces of Córdoba, Jaén, Seville, Almería, Granada, Málaga, Cádiz and Huelva, the last five of which have Mediterranean or Atlantic coastlines. It is crossed in the north by the mountain ranges of the Sierra Morena and in the south by the Sierra Nevada. These protect the region from extremes of weather and give the southern coasts their sub-tropical climate. The ancient inland cities of Granada, Seville and Córdoba are largely commercial or industrial as are the ports of Málaga and Cádiz. All have large residential areas and attract urbanised expatriates.

The coastal resort areas of Andalusia are the Costa de Almería, the Costa del Sol and the Costa de la Luz.

THE COSTA BRAVA

The Costa Brava, which derives its name from its rugged coastline and the mountains behind, starts at Port Bou at the frontier with France and stretches, entirely in Catalonia and the province of Gerona, to the town of Blanes, just 40 miles north-east of Barcelona. Gerona has been touched by many civilisations: Phoenician, Greek, Roman and then Moor, who came, primarily, to use its many natural harbours and sandy bays for shelter from storms and pirates. It was not until the beginning of this century that Gerona became a series of resorts, for artists, writers and the rich from all over Europe and further afield, and today it is a popular cosmopolitan tourist and retirement area.

The Costa Brava has a fairly mild climate with generally low humidity, a year-round temperature range of between 0 and 30°C and comparatively little rain. In addition to the usual seaside sporting activities, within a few hours' drive there is skiing in the Pyrenees. In the tourist high season there are music and art festivals as well as regattas and nautical competitions.

Some of the best known areas along the Costa Brava are Puerto de Llansá, Cadaqués, La Escala, Estartit, Bagur, Palamós, San Feliú de Guixols, Tossa de Mar, Lloret de Mar, and Blanes. The A7 motorway, which links the French frontier with Alicante, passes a few miles inland as do railway lines connecting the Costa Brava with the rest of Spain and all of Europe.

THE COSTA DORADA

The coastline of Tarragona, the southernmost province of Catalonia, is called the Costa Dorada. Here, the ruggedness of the Costa Brava diminishes, the mountains are further inland, there is the vast plain of the Ebro delta and there are the long stretches of the wide golden sandy beaches from which it derives its name. The capital is the important commercial and fishing port of Tarragona which is close to areas of villas, apartments, hotels and camping sites. All along the coast there are tourist developments, mostly beach-side, the best known being those at Sitges, Milagra, Pineda, Cape Salou, Hospitalet and Cambrils. The A7 motorway to Alicante hugs the coast for a large part of the province of Tarragona, turning briefly inland when it reaches the wide delta of the River Ebro, which fans out with narrow tributaries towards rice paddies, irrigation canals and more extensive beaches, many of them lining shallow lagoons. Inland, in addition to the many relics of past civilisations, there are spas and a wide area dedicated to the production of wine. The climate is similar to that of Gerona.

THE COSTA DEL AZAHAR

This coast of orange blossoms stretches from Vinaroz along the Gulf of Valencia as far as Denia, past a number of industrial towns and, as its name implies, vast citrus plantations. There are a number of popular resorts along the Costa del Azahar, amongst them Peñíscola, Oropesa, Cullera and Gandía, all with extensive beaches, although there are parts where the sea may sometimes suffer from industrial pollution. There is little difference in climate from the Costa Dorada and Gerona.

THE COSTA BLANCA

The white sands of its beaches gave this coast its descriptive name. The Costa Blanca stretches from Denia on the Gulf of Valencia to Mazarrón. Here the climate is considered one of the best and most equable in Spain with minimal rainfall, especially in the summer months. The number of popular resorts along this coast has increased rapidly over the past decade and there are many small residential colonies of expatriates from European countries and from North and South America as well as many Spanish families who maintain secondary homes. Amongst the principal residential resort areas are Calpe, Benidorm, Villajoyosa, Moraira and Altea.

THE COSTA CÁLIDA

This coast, which was once considered merely a part of the Costa Blanca, is actually the cooler seaside region of the province of Murcia which, in summer, can often become extremely hot from the winds flowing down from the central plain. The Costa Cálida has a few resorts, amongst them Mar Menor, La Unión, Carbonera and Puerto de Mazarrón. Its principal town is Cartagena, founded by the Carthaginians in 221 BC. It stretches from Cabo de Palos down towards Cabo de Gata.

THE COSTA DE ALMERÍA

Until recently, on its discovery by the ever-increasing number of tourists from northern Europe, this area was considered to be part of the best-known of Spanish coasts, the Costa del Sol. Today, however, from north of Cabo de Gata at the entrance to the Gulf of Almería, the 120-mile stretch of beaches, coves, orchards and vineyards has become a distinct region of small seaside resorts lined by vegetable fields growing several crops a year under plastic covers, desert dunes overlooked in the distance by the Alpujarra mountains with the heights of the often snow-covered Sierra Nevada behind. The Costa de Almería claims 3,000 hours of intensely bright sunshine per year and has long been a centre for experimental solar power-stations. The best-known tourist and residential resorts are at Playa del Palmer, Aguadulce and Roquetas del Mar.

THE COSTA DEL SOL

From the border with Almería to Tarifa, the southernmost town in Europe, in the province of Cádiz, this coast, straddling the city of Málaga, offers 200 miles of beaches, hotels, large apartment blocks, residential villages or *pueblos*, resorts, yacht marinas and golf clubs. It is host to millions of package and independent tourists almost all year round, and is a popular venue for holiday homes and for retirement. The population of the Costa del Sol is cosmopolitan, with numerous nationalities amongst its permanent residents, estimated to number around 25,000, from Europe, North and South America and the Middle East.

The coastal areas have become more crowded and there are now developments in the many attractive inland rural villages, of villas rather than apartments.

The climate is equable but warmer and more humid in all seasons than in the more northerly coastal areas.

Best known of the major resort areas are Nerja, Torremolinos, Fuengirola, Marbella, Nueva Andalucía, Estepona and Sotogrande. Inland, the villages of Coín, Alhaurín el Grande, and

Casares are becoming popular. At La Línea, a gate-less causeway leads past Spanish and British check-points to Gibraltar.

THE COSTA DE LA LUZ

Commencing at the entrance to the Straits of Gibraltar, where the Atlantic joins the Mediterranean, then continuing to the city of Cádiz, there are 80 miles of the tide-washed beaches of the little publicised Costa de la Luz. Until the 1980s, this section of Spain's coastline was virtually unknown to the average visitor and is still comparatively undeveloped. The highway follows the coast a short distance inland, and joins the connecting motorway to the two provincial capitals of Cádiz and Seville.

Of the Costa de la Luz's many beaches, some are long and wide and others short and relatively rocky with low sandstone cliffs. Large, mainly flat, areas of pine woods stretch back from the coastline to the main road and beyond. There are two major developments, at San Andres Golf and a villa urbanisation at Cabo Roche. There are small estates at Barbate de Franco, Conil de la Frontera and the yacht club at Sancti-Petri.

Cádiz is a large port with a naval base and industrial areas. Further north, at the estuary of the river Guadalquivir, which marks the beginning of the province of Huelva is the immense Doñana National Park. The coast from there on to Huelva is virtually undeveloped touristically as far as Mazagón, where there is a large resort hotel. From the mainly industrial city of Huelva, also connected by motorway to Seville, there are a number of small beaches stretching to the River Guadiana at Ayamonte, which is the frontier with Portugal and the beginning of the Algarve.

The Costa de la Luz faces mainly south-west and the climate is similar to the other southern coastal areas of Spain, but fractionally cooler in both summer and winter owing to the effect of the Atlantic breezes.

THE BALEARIC ISLANDS

The archipelago of the Balearic Islands consists of the five islands of Mallorca, Menorca, Ibiza, Formentera and Cabrera, 1,500 square miles in all. Their climate is cooler in summer and milder in winter than on the mainland, mainly owing to the surrounding sea. The terrain of each is similar, with hills and rolling flatlands covered with pine woods. In the north of Mallorca, which is less developed than the eastern coast with its mass tourism resorts, there are mountains rising to nearly 5,000 feet. Each island has rugged coves as well as wide sandy beaches and, whilst tourism is a major industry in all the Balearic Islands, agriculture is important in the level areas. Relics and monuments of previous civilisations abound.

Communications with northern Europe are mainly by air, via Palma (Mallorca) and Mahón (Menorca) international airports. Sea connections are with Barcelona, Alicante, and Valencia. There are also ship services from France, Italy and Algeria, and an inter-island ferry service. Virtually all of the social, sports and relaxation facilities available on the mainland are to be found in each island.

British Banks in the Balearics:

Barclays Bank SAE,
Avenida Alejandro Rosello 15,
07002 Palma de Mallorca

Barclays Bank SAE,
Edificio Alkaid, Portals Nous,
Palma de Mallorca.

THE CANARY ISLANDS

The Canary Islands, with a population of over one and a half million, comprise two provinces of Spain off the north-west coast of Africa: Las Palmas contains the islands of Gran Canaria, Fuerteventura and Lanzarote, and Santa Cruz de Tenerife contains Tenerife, Las Palmas, Gomera and Hierro.

The Islands' climate is sub-tropical, dry and warm throughout most of the year. The landscape, of beaches, mountains, valleys and deserts, volcanic rocks and extinct craters is very varied.

The Canary Islands are served by an international airport at Las Palmas and two in Tenerife. Flight time non-stop from UK airports is just over four hours. There are island-linking air and shipping services. Cruise traffic is considerable and calls are made by major shipping lines serving southern African ports.

Sporting activities are similar to those in the Spanish Mediterranean resorts, but with perhaps more emphasis on water activities such as snorkelling and scuba-diving.

British banks in the Canary Islands are:

Lloyds Bank (London and South America),
Avenida de Anaga 37–39,
38001 Santa Cruz de Tenerife.

Barclays Bank SAE,
Presidente Alvear 25,
Las Palmas.

CEUTA AND MELILLA

Ceuta is a small Spanish enclave of five square miles on the African coast on the south side of the Straits of Gibraltar, and is administered as a part of the province of Cádiz. It is an important port with a ferry service to Algeciras, 16 miles to the north across the Straits. It has a large tourist population in the high season, and is a take-off point for coach tours of northern Moroccan cities. Its small expatriate population is made up largely of employees of shipping and tour companies.

Melilla, slightly smaller than Ceuta, is a port on the Moroccan coast used for the export of iron ore and for fishing and tourism. A narrow isthmus connects it with the mainland. It has been Spanish since 1496 and is administered as part of the province of Granada. It is a popular tourist centre and is connected by ferry with Almería and Málaga. It has a small expatriate population.

Both Ceuta and Melilla are of doubtful popularity as retirement areas.

3
Visa Requirements

The following rules apply to nationals of EEC countries:
Visas are NOT required for visits to Spain of less than 90 days' duration.

For periods longer than 90 days:
Visas are not required for self-employment or for dependent relatives of the self-employed person or for the dependent relatives of an EEC national who is already legally resident in Spain. Visas are required for the purposes of paid employment, residence, extended holiday and study.
Visas are granted by the Consulate General on presentation of:
1   full valid passport with a minimum validity of 180 days, and
2   3 passport-sized photographs, and
3   3 fully completed application forms, and
4   a work contract in the case of paid employment.
Work permits, residence permits and extensions for long holidays and study are granted when in Spain. Applications should be made at the local police station, within 90 days of arrival in Spain.

Visa application forms require the following information:
  1   Surname . . . Married women should give their maiden name (see p.70).
  2   First names. . . .
  3   Present nationality. . . .
  4   Nationality of origin . . . (for those who are not originally of British nationality).
  5   Country. . . . place. . . . and date of birth. . . .
  6   Marital status. . . .

7   Name. . . . and nationality. . . . of husband or wife, in the latter case her maiden name.
8   Profession. . . .   9   Present occupation. . . .
10 Last address in your country of origin. . . .
11 Present address. . . .   Since. . . .
12 Do you have a residence permit. . . . ?   13 If so, until what date. . . . ?
14 Do you have a re-entry permit. . . . ?   15 If so, until what date. . . . ?
16 Passport number. . . .   17 Issued at. . . .
18 By (government office). . . .   19 Date of issue. . . .
20 Type of passport. . . .   21 Valid until. . . .
22 Purpose of visit. . . .
23 Frontier and date of entry. . . .
24 Date and point of departure. . . .
25 Cities you intend to visit and addresses at which you will be staying in each. . . .
26 References in Spain. . . .
27 References in UK. . . .
28 If you have previously visited Spain state date. . . . and reason. . . . for visit.
Place and date of signing. . . .
Signature. . . .

(14 & 15 presumably apply to citizens of countries requiring re-entry permits.)
The completed documents with photographs attached should be taken in person, with the relevant papers, to the Spanish Consulate General, where any questions may be raised. The Consulate General is open on weekdays from 9am until 2pm and on Saturdays from 9am until 12 midday. Visa applications should be lodged before 12 midday.

4
Investing in Property

RENTING BEFORE BUYING

The question of whether to buy immediately or rent for a period before buying, is one which is worth considering. It depends mainly on whether you wish to live permanently in your selected area. Many people, when they retire abroad, prefer to own the roof over their heads outright, and at any cost. Obviously, for these people, anything other than immediate purchase is out of the question; but for others, renting for periods until they decide on a place in which to settle can be very attractive. Not only does it lead to maintenance of mobility, in case you should find that the town, village or neighbours are not quite to your liking or the way of life as you imagined, but with current high interest rates, there is also much financial merit in renting. Interest on the capital required to purchase a house or an apartment can, in many cases, more than provide for rented accommodation and, sometimes, also living expenses, in a similar property, for a reconnaissance visit.

Most estate agents in Spain carry houses or apartments on their books for short and long rental. However, renting is essentially a business directed towards seasonal holiday-makers and usually long-term lets are not easy to find. All new rentals are now subject to recently-imposed controls so that a contract between you and the landlord, overseen by your lawyer, is essential. This should define *inter alia* the exact dates of commencement and expiry of the lease, the price, and any special arrangements you may make.

If you were to plan to take a long lease on a Spanish property and to live there for its duration, it would be advisable to take legal advice as to whether (as you would be subject to Spanish income tax after 183 days) the UK tax authorities might, in due course, accept your residence as an indication of intent which, along with other actions you could take, would qualify you for change of domicile and relief from British income tax.

SELECTING A PROPERTY

By far the best way to select a Spanish property is to decide on the general area to which you are attracted by reading travel books or articles in the Sunday or daily newspapers, and then to visit and tour around it at your leisure in a rented car. In this way, you can see most of the coastal and inland towns or villages, call on estate agents or developers and see what is currently available, learn of what is likely to be available in the near future and, in the case of new properties, compare prices, quality of design and construction and meet people who have been resident for some time.

A rule of thumb for the rapid estimation of the total sterling cost of a property offered is to take the 'transfer' rather than the 'tourist' rate of exchange (this can be obtained from any bank) and then add 15 per cent to cover taxes, legal fees, registration costs and the inevitable small outgoings, plus, to be realistic, the expenses of your viewing visit.

For those without much time to spare on reconnaissance, some UK agents arrange short two-nights-three-days inclusive tours allowing you to do much the same as above, often with the undertaking to refund your air-fare should you purchase from them, but of course these tours are within designated areas. On them you meet English-speaking Spanish estate agents and developers who have business arrangements with their counterparts in Britain and normally there is no pressure on potential clients to make a quick decision. However, there are some tours where 'hard selling' is practised, especially when they are heavily 'escorted'. On these you must remember that properties are not sold but bought and you are the buyer.

BUYING LAND AND BUILDING

When you decide to purchase a plot of land to build on, you are faced with the selection of a site: a single separate plot or one which is contained in a development.

First you must determine whether you wish to be close to a beach, in or near a village, in or adjacent to a fair-sized resort town, or in a rural area, which usually means in the nearby foothills of one of the mountain ranges. All have advantages and drawbacks, and you are best guided by the principal use to which you will put the property as well as personal preferences.

If a property is to be used for your close family's holidays as well as your residence, then proximity to a beach may be very important, but here it is wise to consider the extra maintenance costs of a building subject to salt- and sand-laden sea breezes.

A property in or near a village has advantages with regard to shopping, telephone, mains electricity and water services and the lack of necessity for a personal means of transport.

In the more inland areas, lower land prices may often be counterbalanced by the costs of installing electricity and water supplies if these are not generally available, and a car will be essential.

Land in Spain is always measured and priced by the square metre (1.09 square yards). Internal house areas are also calculated in square metres by adding together the areas of all the rooms and covered balconies. Uncovered terraces are described similarly, but usually separately. Unlike the UK, access to land registers is available and the names of owners of adjacent properties are shown in the deeds.

The fifteen important steps

Once you have decided upon the area and type of purchase, there are fifteen basic sequential steps to be taken from selection to occupation.

1 Visit, reconnoitre, inspect, and decide on a site, alone or in the company of an estate agent.

2 Engage a lawyer to act for you and to check current owner-

ship of your intended purchase and whether there are any encumbrances.

3 Visit the *Ayuntamiento* (town council) with your lawyer to see the area development plan, if appropriate, and any regulations or building requirements that might affect you.

4 If your land choice is in an undeveloped rural area, check with an official surveyor to ensure that you have sources of water and electricity.

5 If your lawyer advises you that there are no zoning or other regulations which will prevent you proceeding, inform the *Ayuntamiento* that you will apply for a building permit as soon as you have purchased the land.

6 Attend the *notario*'s (public notary) office with your lawyer and the current owner of the land and draw up an *escritura de compraventa* (see typical *escritura* p. 40).

7 Visit your bank with the vendor, pay for the property, obtain a bank certificate (see p. 40), return to the *notario* and both you and the vendor sign the *escritura*. The *escritura* is then legalised by the *notario* who, after giving you a '*copia simple*' (a legalised photocopy) will retain the original for registration. As some time will pass before the *escritura* is returned to you via the *notario* it will be best if your lawyer takes the *escritura* immediately to the property registry.

8 As you are now legal owner of the property, you can proceed with building by engaging an architect, preferably a local one who is familiar with the area and is a member of a 'college'. He will either design to your specifications, or adapt plans of your own.

9 Inform him of the type and quality of construction materials and fittings you desire as well as the exact siting of your house on the land. He will then draw the plans and provide a brief, known as a '*memoria*', for a builder. The architect will charge a fee, the amount of which will be relative to the builder's estimated cost of the construction.

10 At this point it is a good idea to apply to the telephone company (*Compañia Telefónica Nacional de España*) for a telephone if one is required, as installation can take some time.

11 The next step is to locate a builder who, again, should be

a member of a 'college'. Your architect is probably the best person to advise you on this as he will want his plans carried out to perfection and to your satisfaction. The builder will quote an 'all-in' price using your materials specifications and, if you insist, a finishing date, usually subject to a *'force majeure'* clause. If the price or the time does not suit you, then there is plenty of competition in the construction industry and you should have no difficulty in obtaining other quotations.

12   Having decided upon a builder, with your lawyer and possibly also your architect having checked over the contract, the method of payment is arranged. Most builders work on the 'stage' system and require an adequate deposit on signing the agreement, and then further percentages of the total cost at various stages of the construction: when the roof is mounted; when the external fittings are completed and the windows ready for glass; when the painting and rendering of the inside walls is finished and when the internal fitments are in place. It has been a custom for a long time for an owner, after negotiation, to withhold a small percentage of the total cost, for a period of up to a year, to ensure attention to any defects which might appear during this time.

13   When the contract is signed you should obtain, usually by recommendation of your architect, an overseer of the construction who is called an *'aparejador'*. He will also be a member of a 'college', a professional with an architectural, building and engineering background, who will check upon the work throughout its progress. He will charge a fee, usually based upon the amount of the architect's charge. He is the person who will certify by means of a *'certificado de habitabilidad'* when your house is finished, that it is ready for electricity meter installation (by the electricity company) and occupation.

14   At this point call with your lawyer at the municipal tax office and register your new house for the *'contribuciones urbanas'*, the equivalent of rates in Britain. This is based on the 'official value' which is usually less than the actual construction cost. From this is calculated a potential annual rental value, a small percentage of which will be the *'contribuciones urbanas'*.

15   The last and most important step is to present yourself with

your lawyer at the *notario's* office and arrange for the house as a new structure to be added to the *escritura* you hold for the land.

Screening
One important point which people from other climes tend to overlook is that much of Spain is agricultural and that tomato fields, olive groves, orchards and onion patches are all conducive to the propagation of the common fly. Thus, in the country areas, for happy mealtimes, drinktimes and bedtimes it is advisable to screen the windows. In high-rise apartments, the highest floors do not seem to attract flying insects.

Builders do not usually install screens as a matter of course, but the cost for all but the largest villas is not great and naturally will be less if the screens are fitted during construction.

With plastic screening now available, such fitments, unlike the metal mesh of yesteryear, last much longer in any climate and require no maintenance other than an occasional brushing.

For the person who finds him or herself in unscreened property and troubled by flying insects, the purchase at the local ironmonger of a few square metres of cheap plastic netting, a packet of drawing pins, and their judicious use over windows or doors, will restore tranquillity.

Landscaping
For the gardening enthusiast there are professional landscape gardeners who, for the owner of a newly-built villa, will rapidly transform the mess of broken tiles, bricks, cement blocks, sand and dust which builders leave behind, into a carefully-planned contoured garden where bougainvillaea, hibiscus, geraniums, marigolds, roses and many other temperate and tropical plants will grow and bloom surprisingly quickly.

Swimming pools
For a large part of the year the Mediterranean is not the warmest of seas, so swimming pools are to be found everywhere in southern Spain: in the grounds of hotels, in the communal lands

of urbanisations, in the gardens of the high-rise apartment blocks and in those of a vast number of private villas.

In most towns there are competent pool construction specialists and shops that market all the latest equipment. They sell circulation pumps, skimmers, chemical injection points and chemicals which ensure that waters are kept clean and bacteria-free, and control acidity or alkalinity so as to maintain the water in peak condition all year—providing, of course, that stray leaves, grass and other contaminants are regularly removed.

Many types of pool heaters are readily available, using heat transfer pumps, electrical pumps and solar power.

BUYING PRE-OWNED VILLAS

In Spain, as elsewhere, the pre-owned house certainly has great advantages over the newly-built, the 'in-construction' and the 'about-to-commence-construction' property. You can see exactly what you are buying, what its immediate surroundings are or are likely to be within the fairly foreseeable future, and the general standard of workmanship, not only in the cement and brickwork, but also in the rendering of the inside walls and ceilings, and fitments. In addition, you can obtain, by examining the services bills of the current owner, an idea of what the annual running costs, taxes or charges are likely to be. In the case of a house over a couple of years old, particularly, you will usually find that any additional work of repairing walls and tile floorings which have 'settled' has been done.

As with new property, you should deal through an accredited estate agent or through a lawyer, or both, even though an owner who wishes to deal directly might increase the price a little to cover the cost of commissions and fees. In this way, you can be sure that the seller is actually the owner or holds a properly registered power of attorney from the owner, you can see the original deed, or deeds if the land and house were sold separately, and you can also estimate the small *'plus valía'* tax (see p. 64; *Plus Valía*) which will be levied by the local authorities when the property changes hands.

Licensed estate agents in Spain are very jealous of their integrity and will usually put all the facts on the table and give a reasonable picture, as far as they know, of the future local development situation.

Property is always sold and bought freehold.

BUYING PRE-OWNED APARTMENTS

You can find modern high-rise apartment blocks, say six to twelve storeys, in most of the major and many of the small, often very small, coastal resorts. Some town councils with jurisdiction over places newly developing are benefiting from the experience of those which are longer established, and strictly limit the number of storeys new buildings may have, in order to preserve much of the sea or mountain views.

If a potential apartment owner merely requires a nicely built place in the sun to retire to, and is not particular about noise, or is impervious to repetitive sounds of discos and bars which might drive some people out of their minds, he or she will have no problem. But popular resorts in Spain, as elsewhere, provide as much night-life as the market will bear and that, especially in the summer months of wide-open windows, is considerable.

One of the most popular forms of modern night entertainment in southern Spain is the indoor or outdoor discothèque. These ultra-modern dance palaces tend to continue their operation until the early hours of the morning, every morning, during the long high season. It is therefore a good idea to ascertain, before purchase, the proximity of all local entertainment centres installed or planned in or adjacent to the location of one's potential property.

Another point to bear in mind is proximity to a main road or to a corner where a minor road meets a traffic flow. Much of Spain's voluminous truck traffic moves at night and the heavy diesel trucks are not noted for their quietness nor for their freedom from fumes.

Proximity to traffic lights should also be considered, as the crashes of gear changes of ten-ton vehicles pulling away from the signals can be compared only with the brakes screeching as they come to a stop.

Also worth investigation is the noise made by lifts in an apartment building. In a flat on or near the top floor or *ático*, as it is called, you will frequently find that you will hear every movement of the lifts, whose motors are located on the roof. In some older buildings, the gates installed in the elevators make even more sound. These points are well worth looking into before a decision is made.

A check on the type and efficiency of ceiling and wall sound-proofing is also to be recommended, as few people really like to be made aware of every move made by neighbours on each side, above and below.

Water pressure in apartments can produce problems especially if, as is often the case, small-gauge pipes have been used. In some buildings, the higher the apartment the lower the water pressure and, in such cases, when a gas water heater is located some distance from the bathroom, you can wait a considerable time for a bath to fill; ergo also check the size of the water pipes.

Some of the complaints made by people who have bought apartments in Spain have been related to the 'here-today-gone-tomorrow' views. Many purchasers decide upon a property because of the sea or mountain vistas from the windows and balconies, only to find that within a short time, other buildings have been erected in front and at the sides and that their picture windows now look merely upon other identical accommodations and the laundry of their occupants. The charming scenes of field after field of tomatoes or green beans stretching along the coast or away to the snow-covered high sierras are almost certain in time, as the value of the land becomes greater than its productive potential for agriculture, to be built upon. Similarly, although a building may seem at one moment to be so close to the beach that the sea view is unobstructable, one must always reckon with the ingenuity of developers who can, and frequently do, find a way to squeeze yet another building in front. There is a saying that the only way to ensure unobstructed views in Spain is to build on the edge of a precipice or on stilts over the sea itself!

URBANISATIONS

The word 'urbanisation' is used loosely in Spain to describe any development, but usually refers to one on the edge of a town or village. 'Development' is used in the same context, and often also *'pueblo'*, where the overall lay-out and design reproduces in some form the look of a typical small Andalusian village (see p. 32)

In urbanisations land is usually sold with the proviso that a house will be built upon it and completed within a certain period, and in many cases, that the construction will be undertaken by the developer selling the plot.

Before a promoter may place his planned urbanisation on the market he must install roads, electricity, water mains and sewers. Often he may place these services in a small portion of the total intended development area, at first, so that the proceeds from the sale of the plots and the houses or villas which he builds on them, will contribute towards the placing of services on the remainder of the land. You should, therefore, ascertain, before buying a plot of land or a finished house, what the size will be of the completed urbanisation. Otherwise, you might easily find that the relatively secluded house surrounded by a few others of equal charm eventually turns out to be just one of hundreds of similar structures that, in toto, can best be described as a suburb of the nearest town.

Sometimes houses or flats in urbanisations are sold on the principle of the 'buyer finances a developer', by which a purchaser selects his property from a prospectus illustrated by artists' impressions, and then contracts to pay in instalments whilst the construction is being carried out on the 'stage' system. On occasion, a 'show' house or apartment is finished and furnished so as to indicate the quality and appearance of the completed work. In the case of an apartment in a large building, or one of a group of houses, the 'buyer finances a developer' method can produce delays before completion for the first buyers to sign, as the developer may well have to sell and obtain down payments on some or all of the others in the group before he can commence construction.

You may find that in some urbanisations, a large proportion of houses are rented at times to holiday-makers, especially in the peak vacation periods of June to September and Christmas and Easter. In these periods such places can cease to be relaxing havens for retirement, and with most habitations full, they can become more like the holiday camp of yester-year. At such times, of course, a variety of communal services, especially swimming pools, are stretched to the limit and nights tend to be bathed in cacophony as well as moonlight.

Permanent residents then often go elsewhere, but for those who prefer to spend the holiday seasons in their own homes, careful checking before purchase as to the number of houses that are actually for rent at any time is advisable. Such research can perhaps be done most reliably by consulting owners already in residence, as well as the promoters.

It is important to remember that the purchase of a property in a development complex entitles the buyer to the use of a number of amenities such as gardens, stairways and private roads, which are for the sole use of the residents as well as, in many cases, compliance with the 'green belt' laws designed to control population and housing density. Amenities such as these are known as communal lands when registered as such and when the owners contribute to their upkeep. They are valuable parts of your property. Their ownership should be clearly stated in the title deed in order to avoid any confusion which might occur at the completion of the urbanisation if they were still owned by the developing company.

Urbanisations are obliged to practise a form of self-regulation through what is called a 'Community of Owners'. There must be regular and at least annual meetings of all owners in a development, whether it be in a block of apartments or in an agglomeration of villas. There must be 'statutes' or 'articles of association' and the election, from amongst the owners, of a chairman usually called a *'presidente'*. He will be responsible for the efficient running of the community and the services which are provided for the owners. This work is generally carried out by means of an employed administrator paid for out of the annual charges agreed at the meetings and collected from the owners on a monthly, quarterly or annual basis. These charges cover the costs of maintenance of such communal benefits as internal roads and their lighting, gardens, swimming pools, and often water charges where use is not metered at the consumption points in dwellings. In addition there may be further charges for the regular exterior painting of buildings when required by the statutes. The administrator keeps track of all community matters and progress on association resolutions, and reports to the *presidente* who, in turn, informs the association.

Example of annual charges

This example is based on hypothetical annual charges on an apartment in a development of 26 similarly-sized units, and where there is not a paid administrator:

Gardener (12 months at pt 40,000 per month)	480,000
Extra months (July and December)	80,000
Social security (employer's contribution)	183,436
Water consumption for gardens	82,250
Electricity consumption for street lighting	98,365
Chemical fertilisers	19,000
Repairs to mowing machine	50,970
Petrol for mowing machine	14,800
Maintenance of other equipment	21,560
	1,030,381
Administration charges at 10 per cent	103,038
	1,133,419
Charge to each apartment at 1/26 of total	43,593

If the apartments were of different sizes then the total area in square metres of all the apartments would be calculated and the owners charged in proportion to the number of square metres owned by each.

In addition to community charges, owners pay the '*contribución urbana*' (rates) and sometimes are liable for small municipal taxes as well as a charge for rubbish collection and of course for their own consumption of electricity and water.

Some people might find community charges, in relation to what one might pay a British local council for rates and taxes, to be often unrealistic. It is perhaps preferable to find out before buying or building in an urbanisation, just what the charges have been over the previous year or years and what they might be in the future.

For those with a well-developed sense of community spirit, who like organised social centres and regular neighbourly get-togethers, there may be no better place to reside than in one of the many well-organised urbanisations, even though it may mean submitting to rules and regulations and paying annual charges decided upon by a majority of votes at meetings of a multi-national association of owners.

However, if you don't consider this to be an attractive way of life, and would prefer to choose your own social circle, or if you like to make individual decisions as to the time and manner of redecorating the exterior of your house or prefer not to use the services of a corps of gardeners and do your own pottering amongst the local flora, then a dwelling that comes within the jurisdiction of a local *Ayuntamiento* (town council) for services can be a better choice. In such an area, owners pay '*contribución urbana*' or rates, and any small local taxes, to the *Ayuntamiento*.

Security

Security of property is taken very seriously in all urbanisations. The larger ones usually have their own, sometimes uniformed, patrols which operate day and night and are paid for from the annual charges. Some have a sort of guardhouse at the gate to check on people entering and leaving, and all are patrolled by the local police and often by the provincial forces as well.

All public roads are regularly patrolled by the *Guardia Civil* and rural police forces.

There is no emergency telephone system, equivalent to the UK's 999, as yet.

Houses in '*pueblos*'

In recent years, a type of urbanisation known as a '*pueblo*' has become much sought-after by persons looking for a home in Spain. Based roughly on the overall look of the small mountain villages that dot, in great numbers, the hinterland of the southern coastline, the typical, modernised *pueblo* is a group of one- and two-storey houses built in the traditional style with white walls and reddish-brown tiled gutterless roofs, lining small, quiet, sometimes cloistered streets and cobbled lanes. Bright sunlight, deep cool shadows, low-walled flowering gardens and miniature tree-shaded plazas, often with small fountains, combine to produce the overall effect of this type of development. Traffic does not enter, cars are parked along the perimeter, electricity wires are underground as in other types of development, and where there are small restaurants and bars, they are inconspicuous, almost hidden in the overall façade.

Except for the cobblestones, which many urban northerners find somewhat noisy and uncomfortable to walk upon, a properly-administered *pueblo* can provide as much peace and quiet and gentle gracious living as one could wish.

Town houses

Town houses are a relatively new type of development. Usually they are small, two-storeyed terrace houses built in rows of a dozen or so, with very small walled gardens at front and rear. Their main advantages are: a builder can obtain more residential square footage out of a piece of land than with other styles; they are cheaper, simpler and quicker to construct; and their services are less expensive to install. For the purchaser, they are often cheaper to acquire, easier to maintain, cooler in summer owing to the reduced number of outside walls, and, for the same reason, warmer in winter.

Villas

Most villas are bungalows, but there are also many attractive split-level designs. Developers usually offer their plot purchasers a choice of half a dozen designs for which they already have the architects' plans and for which they can quote a firm price and a fairly firm, depending on how much one insists, completion date. Much construction is done on the piece-work principle, with the result that some houses are built remarkably quickly. One should, however, take the precaution of insisting that the contract includes a delivery delay penalty clause.

One can settle for one of the standard plans of the builder, or engage a local architect to design just what is required. The architect's fee will, of course, increase the total cost. Although construction systems in Spain are, in many ways, different from those in other countries, there is no reason why one should not, as thousands have done, have one's own ideas translated expertly into exactly the type of building one desires. It is mainly a question of a good architect and a good builder—and sometimes great patience and abundant *savoir-faire*.

The principal internal differences between Spanish, or at any rate Andalusian, houses and those which one finds in countries further north are: the sizes of the rooms, the height of the ceilings and the dimensions of such built-in essentials as shelves, cupboards, kitchen counters, bathroom fittings and windows. Northern Europeans often seem to find that the standard ceilings and fittings are far too low for comfort and use.

OLD RURAL HOUSES

From time to time, in recent years, usually in places somewhat distant from the mass tourist centres, very old houses, called '*fincas*' or often, if with considerable adjoining land, '*cortijos*', and usually in need of renovation, have come on to the market. These are much sought after as invariably their construction and situation have stood the test of time. They have been well built and positioned by local families, usually '*campesinos*' who worked in the surrounding lands, so that maximum benefit is obtained from year-round climatic conditions. They are likely to be warm in winter, cool in summer and naturally protected from wind and weather by trees or terrain. For the imaginative active person they are ideal for interior and exterior transformation into desirable residences, hence their popularity amongst knowledgeable seekers of houses in rural areas.

The cost of '*plus valía*' on these properties should be carefully checked by your lawyer prior to purchase (see p. 64, Taxes—Plus Valía).

TIME-SHARING

In an ingenious move to sell up-market properties, a French company, a decade or so ago, commenced selling what they called '*Multiples Vacances*', where they offered the tenure of apartments and, in some cases, villas for annual weekly periods over a fixed number of years for a single payment plus annual maintenance costs. Thus, a person not able to afford an apartment in a fashionable watering place could, for a fraction of the purchase price, own and use a holiday home for one week or more over a number of years, in some cases in perpetuity. It was looked upon as a simple method of dealing with the regular increase in resort hotel prices. The apartments were sold on a per-week basis, with prices highest for those wishing to use them during the major holiday periods and lowest during the off-seasons. One could buy any number of weeks, consecutive or spread over the year. The scheme benefited the purchasers as well as the developers, who were able to finance construction costs.

People who felt that they did not perhaps wish to visit the same place at the same time every year, were able to let their ownership periods to relatives or friends, or through normal business channels, and use the proceeds to go elsewhere at a time of their own choosing. In time, as the system grew, it became possible for such changes to be arranged and handled by a rental clearing house which collected fees for the work involved. The system became known as 'time-sharing'.

'Time-sharing' appears to be a simple way to beat inflation, but there are several factors to be borne in mind. Firstly, the annual maintenance costs, which will be governed by inflation in the plumbing, painting, electrical and other industries. Secondly, there is a fee for the use of the exchange services, and thirdly, but perhaps most important, the question of proof of ownership. A firm contract with the developer is important, but 20 or more years is a long time and the company might be sold to another firm, taken over or go bankrupt.

Owing to numerous complaints concerning the selling methods of some time-share developers, a British member of the European Parliament is engaged with others in an investigation into the time-share business and is proposing EEC regulations to control it.

Anyone considering entering into a time-sharing arrangement should follow the advice given by the British Government in a leaflet recently published by the Central Office of Information, and consult a lawyer before paying a deposit or signing any documents.

CO-OWNERSHIP

The concept of co-ownership has been developed from that of time-sharing and eliminates the contractual obligations for maintenance and other charges beyond the control of the unit purchaser.

Co-ownership is a means by which two to four persons purchase a property, each having the use of it and the ability to rent it to others, for a period of three to six months each year. It is a system most suitable for families or close friends. Usage periods, rather than being permanently fixed, as in time-sharing, can be changed at any time by mutual arrangement.

Maintenance costs and timing are controlled entirely by the co-owners, and not by the decisions of a management company servicing up to 52 unit owners of each property, as in time-sharing.

Although time-sharing allows one to let the purchased period and go on vacation in another affiliated property instead using a central property exchange agency, co-owners can obtain a rental return and be free to go anywhere without exchange agency charges. Co-ownership is particularly popular with large families with retired grandparents. The junior family members use the property for their summer vacation breaks, and the grandparents enjoy the winter warmth and sun. Vacant periods can produce an income which contributes towards the upkeep.

Co-ownership has none of the drawbacks of buying a part of a multi-owned property as co-owners are registered in the deed and remain in charge of all running costs at all times.

Co-ownership is actual ownership supported by a registered deed.

PURCHASE OF FIXED PROPERTY

The fundamental rule in Spanish law governing the conveyance of fixed property (real estate) is that conveyance can only be completed by means of a notarial deed (*escritura*) executed by the vendor in favour of the purchaser, in the presence of a Spanish notary. Once the transfer taxes have been paid to the Spanish revenue, the *escritura* is registered in the name of the purchaser, giving the purchaser title to the property in question.

The Land Registry Office provides certificates which indicate whether the property is unencumbered, which prevents problems arising after the transfer of the property.

In certain areas of Spain a 'Good Conduct' certificate may be required before a property can be purchased. This certificate should be issued by a lawyer or Commissioner for Oaths on headed paper which must be legalised by the Spanish Consulate General.

For the person who has little or no knowledge of Spanish, translations of all documents relating to the transaction, made and stamped by an official translator, are well worth the comparatively small cost. Any *Gestoria* can put you in touch with an official translator.

To engage a lawyer, it is perhaps best to consult one's own consulate or embassy, which should be able to provide a list of Spanish lawyers who are known to speak and do business in English. These, as your government representative will not fail to point out, are not vouched for, but you may be certain that all of them will cherish being and remaining on such a list and will render the best possible service.

Investing in Property

THE PUBLIC NOTARY (*NOTARIO*)

The *notario* is an official who is charged with attesting to signatures on legal documents. He ensures that any transaction involving a change of ownership of a property is properly executed and registered according to law. He is a member of a 'College' or professional association of *notarios* and is paid, in the case of a property transfer, a fee based upon the value of the property.

All property transfer deeds and contracts are required to be signed in front of a *notario* who will then attend to the various registration formalities.

THE '*GESTOR*'

A considerable amount of paperwork, registration, tax stamping and document progression through a number of different government departments is required for almost any important transaction to be finalised in a legal manner. Documentation not only takes time but also requires a certain amount of walking, queueing and waiting on the part of the individual who personally undertakes it. It is not a popular pastime in the easy-going way of life in Spain with either Spaniards or foreigners, and for the latter can be exhausting, especially if they have no knowledge of the locations of the government departments concerned. If they also lack a proficient knowledge of the language, in spite of the limitless patience which Spaniards have for the ignorant stranger in their midst, they will soon find themselves looking around for an easier way of achieving their objective.

However, there is always a solution at hand: in every community there is a qualified person, who like the *notario* is a member of a 'College' or professional association. He is known as a '*gestor*', and his office is called a '*Gestoría*'. He is not an official nor necessarily a lawyer, but he and his highly-skilled staff are well versed in all requirements of the law in relation to almost any transaction and have an intimate knowledge of the location and internal geography of all government offices. For a relatively small fee plus government stamp costs, a '*gestor*' will attend correctly and expeditiously to all sorts of business: the registration of a new motor car, or the obtaining of a residence permit or a driving licence.

The *'gestor'* and the public notary known as the *'notario'* are the two professionals who can smooth the way of the new resident and property owner.

5
Paying for Your Property

A foreigner seeking to buy a property in order to take up residence in Spain must pay for it in pesetas obtained by the exchange of foreign currency at a bank in Spain. If, at a later date, he or she sells this property for pesetas and does not wish to continue to be resident, he or she can obtain foreign exchange for the proceeds up to the amount he or she paid originally. The key to the successful conclusion of this operation for the resident is that, not only must he or she have paid originally by the importation of foreign currency which he or she has exchanged for pesetas, but he or she must also be able to prove that this has been done, by means of a bank certificate which the *notario* will record along with the deed. What must be avoided, as many people have found to their cost, is using a foreign currency cheque, a peseta cheque not backed by evidence of exchange of foreign currency, or foreign cash or pesetas. A receipt from the seller, unsupported by proof of foreign currency conversion through a bank in Spain, is insufficient. Pesetas purchased outside Spain similarly would not qualify.

The best and quickest way to pay for any property you buy is by using a previously opened sterling foreign currency account funded by imported sterling with a bank near to the place where you have chosen to live. It would then be a matter of going with the vendor to your bank manager, stating your intention of paying for the property in sterling and giving the bank a cheque drawn on your foreign currency account for the peseta equivalent of the price. The bank will give the vendor a peseta cheque and you will receive the certificate attesting to the importation of the foreign funds for attachment by the *notario* to the *escritura*.

You will then attend the office of the *notario* with your lawyer and you and the vendor will sign the *escritura*. The *notario* then attaches the bank certificate to the *escritura*, legalises the document and makes a photocopy (a '*copia simple*') for you to hold as evidence of the transaction until registration in the Land Registry is completed.

MORTGAGES

Long-term mortgages of the 25- to 30-year variety popular in the UK are not easy for foreigners to obtain from Spanish sources. However, some developers are increasingly advertising a variety of long-term payment plans for potential purchasers of their properties, sometimes for up to 10 years or more. They are usually based on a substantial deposit followed by monthly or quarterly payments of the balance, with interest on the outstanding amount after each payment, calculated at slightly above the current bank rate. Purchasers are required to sign a series of post-dated promissory notes known as '*letras*', one for each payment. The property is the collateral, so the buyer does not receive his *escritura* (deed) until the final payment of instalments.

Since the entry of Spain into the European Economic Community, a number of British banks have opened branches in Madrid and in some of the resort areas and these might be approached for mortgage funds.

EXAMPLE OF A TYPICAL DEED

Deeds are detailed, but whether they are for land, an apartment or a villa, they contain similar basic details. A typical Spanish deed for a property will be made on the headed notepaper of the *notario* before whom both parties sign, or their representatives holding legalised powers of attorney. (In the case of a joint purchase by husband and wife it is essential that each signs the deed.) Your lawyer would be in attendance.

Firstly, there will be the name and address of the *notario* and his authority to convey the property by being a member of a professional society of members of the same profession, known as a 'College'. There will follow a statement confirming the appearance before him of the seller, with his name, address, marital status, profession and the number of his identity card. Thirdly, there will be the same details of the purchaser and the number of his passport.

There will then be a statement that the seller is the owner of the land which is described: its area in square metres, followed by details of its boundaries to the north, south, east and west and the names of the owners of these contiguous properties, plus notes of any roads or high tension wires which may cross the property.

This is followed by details of the current registration of the land giving the numbers of the section, book and page at the Registry.

Then there will be stipulated:

1 That the land is transferred to the full control of the buyer, free of any debts or rental agreements and that the taxes on the property are paid to date.
2 The purchase price, in words, and acknowledgement that it has been received by the seller.
3 A statement that money paid was obtained by exchange of foreign currency and that a bank certificate to this effect is attached to the deed.
4 That all the expenses of the transmission will be paid by the buyer, including the registration fees, *plus valía* and transmission tax or IVA (VAT).

The final paragraph is a statement that the deed has been read by seller, buyer and *notario* and that it is approved and signed and given legal status.

THE BANK CERTIFICATE

This is obtained by the purchaser with his lawyer and the vendor and is on headed bank paper and prefaced by the name and rank of the person signing on behalf of the bank. It certifies that, on the date given, the bank has received from the seller a cheque in his or her favour for x pounds sterling which the bank has exchanged for y pesetas at the exchange rate of z.

It then states that, following instructions received from the seller of the property, the imported funds have been applied to an investment in fixed property, namely the acquisition of the land named in the deed. Further, that the transfer has been notified to the Bank of Spain and, for this reason, the certificate is issued and dated.

After signature, the *notario* will send the deed with the bank certificate attached to the Central Land Registry. In due course, it will be returned to the owner via the *notario*. In the meantime, the owner obtains from the *notario* a legalised photocopy of the deed and attachment. This is the '*copia simple*' and is the new owner's proof of purchase up until the original is returned by the registration authorities.

PURCHASE OF A HOUSE BY STAGE PAYMENTS

When a house is purchased by stage payments from a developer, prior to the signing of an *escritura* at the completion of the construction, a sale contract is drawn up between the parties. Typically it will contain the name and details of the vendor and of the development company which he is representing, and secondly, a declaration in which the vendor affirms the company as the legal owner of plot number *xyz* of *polígono abc* at a place named, and that the company possesses the title deed made by the notary Don Soandso of (town) on such and such a date. The company is building on this plot a project of h houses under the name *xxxx* and under the direction of architect Don Someonelse.

Stipulations

1 The contract refers to house number 43 B (second floor centre).
2 A brief description of the house is: two bedrooms, dining room, kitchen with covered patio, bathroom and terrace. The area is 93 square metres.
3 Each house in the project is entitled to a share of the communal elements of the project and the development.

4   The house is sold with vacant possession for first occupation by the purchaser.

5   The vendor sells the aforementioned house to the purchaser free of all liens and obligations and with all judgements paid in full to the date of acceptance of the house by the purchaser.

6   The price of the house is pta 000000 (in figures and words) which the purchaser will pay to the vendor in the following fashion: (a) upon signing this document the amount of ptas 000000 (50 per cent) paid with a cheque in pounds sterling (£00000); (b) once the outside and inside walls are finished pta 000000 (25 per cent), and (c) the balance of ptas 000000 (25 per cent) upon completion.

7   The vendor will complete the construction of the house before the end of (date) with a maximum period of grace in the event of '*force majeure*' of three months.

8   In addition to the above it shall be incumbent on the purchaser to pay for notarial work, costs of transfer taxes resulting from this purchase, together with water, electricity and urbanisation charges related to this house.

9   The vendor will transfer the house to the purchaser directly after making the 'declaration of *obra nueva*' and upon having received the total purchase price.

10 The purchaser agrees that he may not convey the rights acquired under this contract until the total purchase price has been paid, except with the vendor's express consent in writing.

11 Should any disagreement arise between the contracting parties, each agrees to accept the jurisdiction of the Judiciary and Courts of (named Spanish town)

SIGNED (vendor) (date) (purchaser)

The purchaser, his lawyer and vendor then visit the purchaser's bank and obtain a bank certificate as in the case of the deed (above) and then legalise the contract before a notary.

Subsequent payments must be made so as to obtain a bank certificate for each. These will be attached to the deed by the *notario* when it is signed upon completion of the contract.

In cases where a house is paid for by instalments over x number of years before the buyer takes up formal residence, the contract will be similar in substance, but will also contain clauses showing the interest rate which the buyer will pay on the balance owing after each payment. Generally, the purchaser will sign a post-dated promissory note or bill of exchange for each instalment plus interest and instruct his bank to pay them in pesetas converted from his sterling account as they become due and to issue a bank certificate for each, which will be attached to the deed when it is signed (as above). There might be another clause requiring the purchaser or vendor to adjust in cash, at the end of the term, any shortfall or excess in the peseta value of the payments due to fluctuations in the exchange rate.

6
Banking in Spain

BANKING BEFORE RESIDENCE

Spanish currency is the peseta, abbreviated to 'pta'. Notes are in denominations of 10,000, 5,000, 2,000, 1,000, 500, 200 and 100 ptas. Coins have values of 1, 2, 5, 10, 25 and 100 pta.

Anyone who is not a resident of Spain is able to open and maintain current or deposit accounts in ordinary pesetas, convertible pesetas, sterling or in any other major currency, with banks in Spain. Funds from convertible pesetas and other currency accounts may be freely transferred out of Spain.

Accounts in ordinary pesetas are available to non-residents, but it must be borne in mind that funds from these accounts cannot be transferred out of Spain. Pesetas earned in Spain may be credited to them, however.

Convertible pesetas accounts may be credited only with funds transferred from outside Spain or with pesetas which have been designated as convertible by the Spanish Exchange Control authorities. Convertible pesetas are usually held in either current accounts or on a fixed deposit basis, the latter with a minimum term of six months and a minimum balance of ptas 1,000,000 (say £5,000 at an exchange rate of ptas 200 to £1 sterling). In certain cases, where the amounts involved so warrant, it may be possible to open 'call' deposit accounts in convertible pesetas. The amounts would usually be for at least ptas 250,000 (£1,250) and this minimum balance would have to be maintained for a substantial period.

Deposit accounts in other currencies earn interest according to the amount deposited, the terms of the deposit (minimum term fixed at one month) and the current market rates. It is general practice for a bank to renew deposits for the same term unless it receives instructions to the contrary.

If you visit Spain as a tourist whilst seeking a suitable retirement residence it could be useful for later transactions when you decide to purchase a property, to establish relations with a Spanish bank before you go by opening one of the above accounts with a bank with branches in the UK. This is a relatively simple matter requiring the completion of two forms, plus authentication of your signature by your British bank, a photocopy of pages 1 to 5 of your passport, funds for the opening of the account and the address of the branch of the bank in Spain at which you wish to place your account. This would probably be at the base from which you decide to conduct your reconnaissance. It could be changed at a later date if necessary.

Opening of non-resident accounts in Spanish banks

Type of account requested
Name of holder
Name of father
Date of birth
Marital status
Domicile
Passport number
Date of issue

Town
Occupation

Name of mother
Country
Nationality

Signature
Signature confirmation

Passport issued at .... by ....

When you have decided on the account and the town at which you want it opened, you ask the London branch of the bank you have selected to send you request forms. Upon completion, these should be returned with a sterling London-cleared draft made payable to the bank, plus your instructions.

Spanish banks in London

Banco de Bilbao, 100 Cannon Street, EC4.

Banco Central, Triton Court, Finsbury Square, EC2.

Banco Exterior UK, 60 London Wall, EC2.

Banco de Jerez, 27 Wood Street, EC2

Banco de Sabadell, 64 Queen Street, EC4.

Banco de Vizcaya, 58 Moorgate, EC2.

Banco Pastor, 88 High Holborn, WC1.

Banco de Santander, 10 Moorgate, EC2.

Banco Urquijo Hispano Americano, 15 Austin Friars, EC2

Banco de Galicia, 41 Crutched Friars, EC3.

Confederacion Española de Cajas de Ahorros, 50 Pall Mall, SW1.

As a visitor, you will be able to take into Spain any amount of foreign currency in notes or travellers' cheques and any amount of pesetas in banknotes. You may take out up to ptas 100,000 (£500) per person in Spanish bank notes, and foreign currency up to the equivalent of ptas 500,000 (£2500), unless you can show that an excess of this amount was declared at Customs when entering the country.

Transfer of funds

Spanish banks in London will transfer sterling to your accounts in Spain by mail or telex as required.

Typical transfer fees quoted by one bank (at time of writing) are:

BY MAIL	Up to £2000 To its branches: no charge. To other banks: £5
	Over £2000 £1.25 per thousand (minimum £5, maximum £30)
BY TELEX	Up to £2000 To branches and other banks £10

Over £2000   £1.50 per thousand
(minimum £10, maximum £30)

Charge and credit cards

Most major charge and credit cards are accepted in many hotels, restaurants and shops after electronic reference.

Holders of accounts and cheque cards of the National Girobank are able to purchase by mail, at a cost of 50 pence each in advance, in books of ten, 'Postcheques' which may be cashed at Spanish post-offices. They should be written in pesetas to the maximum value of £65 per cheque, at the day's rate, but more than one may be cashed at a time. There is no commission payable at the time of cashing nor when your Giro account is debited in the UK.

In major resorts there are cash machines by which some charge card holders with 'PIN' numbers may draw, in local currency, up to the equivalent of £350 per day.

British banks in Spain

Since Spain joined the European Economic Community a number of British banks have opened offices and branches in Madrid and in the resorts most popular with British tourists.

BANK OF LONDON AND SOUTH AMERICA, LTD.

Head Office:
   Calle Serrano 90, 28006 Madrid

Branches:
   Madrid: Calle Serrano 90, 28006 Madrid
   Barcelona: Rambla de Cataluña 123, 08008 (Barcelona)
   Sabadell: Calle Sol 1. Sabadell (Barcelona)
   Marbella: Calle 3b, Nueva Andalucía, Marbella (Málaga)
   Seville: Plaza Nueva 8, 41001 (Sevilla)
   Valencia: Apartado Postal 198, 46080 (Valencia)

BARCLAYS BANK SAE.

Head Office:
Plaza de Colón 1, Madrid 28080

Branches:
Alicante: Alfonso El Sabio 43, 03001 (Alicante)
Barcelona: Paseo de Gracia 45, 08007 (Barcelona)
Benalmádena Costa: Edificio Comercial Ole, 29630 Benalmádena (Málaga)
Fuengirola: Avenida Suel, Puebla Lucia, Edif, Marja Liisa, Fuengirola (Málaga)
Las Chapas: Pueblo Los Arcos, Las Chapas, Marbella (Málaga)
Marbella: Avenida Ricardo Soriano 66, Marbella (Málaga)
Mijas Costa: Edificio Calypso 2, Urb Calypso, Mijas Costa (Málaga)
Nueva Andalucía: Edificio Iberico, Nueva Andalucía (Málaga)
San Pedro de Alcántara: Urb Guadalmina Alta, San Pedro de Alcántara (Málaga)
Sotogrande: Cortijo Los Canos, Sotogrande, San Roque (Cádiz)
Cartagena: Puerta de Murcia 26 Cartagena (Murcia)
Murcia: Plaza de Santa Isabel 9, 30004, Murcia (Murcia)
Seville: Tetuan 32, 41001 (Sevilla)
Moraira: Ctra de Teulada, Km. 5.7, Teulada (Alicante)
Valencia: Apartado de Correos 10, 46002 (Valencia)
Zaragoza: Joaquín Costa 2, 50001 (Zaragoza)

BANKING AFTER YOU BECOME RESIDENT

Once you have taken up residence you will no longer be able to hold non-resident accounts which you might have previously opened. You will use a normal domestic peseta current account for any payments you make in Spain. This account can be funded by credits obtained by foreign currency deposits such as pensions or dividends from the UK which the bank will exchange at the rate of the day upon receipt. It is not freely convertible, but residents are permitted to purchase foreign currency for specific purposes each year to cover such items as vacation travel, medical treatment or hospitalisation, should you need to travel to Britain or elsewhere for them, education costs of any student children and payments to certain dependants living abroad. Each of these items has an annual limit as to the total currency which may be exchanged and, in some cases, accounts may be required in support. Of course, transportation costs which can be pre-paid in pesetas in Spain are not included in the totals for each item. Your local *Gestoría* will be able to advise as to the current allowances for each purpose.

Unlike in Britain, banks pay a small percentage interest on average balances of current accounts. They do not encourage overdrafts and they offer a variety of savings accounts. There are also savings banks which invest their funds in the construction of residential or office buildings in the same way as building societies in the UK. They accept monies on sight withdrawal and on term deposit. The former attract a low rate of interest, but the longer the term the higher the rate.

Banking hours nationally are 9 am until 2 pm from Monday to Friday and 9 am to 1 pm on Saturdays, except on national public holidays

Cheques are called '*talones*' or more usually now '*cheques*' and expire after six months. As many people still do not have bank accounts, cheques made out to small tradesmen are frequently marked to the bearer '*al portador*', literally 'the carrier'. Payments made in cash are called '*en efectivo*'.

As in Britain, exchange rates are displayed at the entrance to the bank. Foreign banknotes are exchanged at one rate, travellers' cheques at a higher rate and personal cheques drawn on a foreign bank, which can sometimes be cashed when you are well-known to the manager, at the transfer rate which can be still higher except, of course, in the case of a small amount.

At each foreign exchange transaction you are given, in duplicate, a slip which shows the date, the type of currency exchanged, the amount, the commission and the total of the small tax. Occasionally when using a bank in a small town or village, you may be asked for your name, address and passport number, which are then marked on the exchange slip.

Banking in Spain

Some large branches of banks operate a system whereby a customer wishing to cash a cheque first goes to one counter where he hands it in and receives in exchange a numbered slip of paper. He waits while the processing takes place and then, when a clerk at another counter calls out the number on his slip, receives his cash from him.

Banking is always conducted with great dignity and politeness. Anyone seeking information or wishing to consult a manager is invariably invited to a private office or to one of the desks in the banking hall where, comfortably seated, business can be dealt with.

Statements of account are rendered monthly or quarterly and carry as much information as in other countries.

7
Public Services and Utilities

TELEPHONES

Throughout almost all of Spain there is an automatic telephone service connected by direct dialling (STD) with the whole of Europe and most of the world, by the National Telephone Company. Bills are mailed approximately every two months. It is not difficult to have a telephone connected, but when a house or apartment is new or pre-owned with a line already installed, application must be made by the new owner through the local office of the *Compañía Telefónica Nacional de España*. Usually, at least two months can elapse between application and installation. The Company offers a variety of instruments including touch button machines, in various colours, extensions, and also telex and land lines. Most directories cover the whole of a province with each city, town or village listed separately under its name. When using the directory you need not be surprised if you are unable to find the number of, say, a restaurant, as you may eventually discover that it is still listed under the name of the person who first had the line installed, possibly many years ago. The service in most places is efficient and the cost comparable with the rest of Europe. Conference and reversed charge calls are also available.

Public telephones
There are numerous public telephone boxes in most Spanish towns and villages, from which one can make trunk and international calls. Those marked '*internacional*' are for communi-

Public Services and Utilities

cation with foreign countries and those with an *'interurbano'* sign for calls to numbers in Spain.

Costs per unit (known as a *'paso'*) are shown in each box on a wall-mounted tariff listing most countries. Each unit charge entitles the caller to speak for a specified number of seconds, the further the distance of the country called, the fewer the number of seconds contained in the unit. A three-minute call to a foreign country usually totals to a number of *pasos* which will cost about the same as a three-minute call from that country to Spain, allowing for variations of exchange rates. The minimum time of a call is one *paso*, a few seconds.

To make an overseas call, one inserts one or a number of coins into a 'feeder lane' at the top of the equipment, lifts the receiver, waits for the dialling tone, dials 07 for the foreign service tone, dials the international code for the country called (for the UK it is 44), and then the STD code and the number required. For calls to Britain from abroad, the zero in front of an STD code number should always be omitted; thus London, code 01, is dialled as 1, followed by the number. For calls to a number in another Spanish province it is necessary to dial the number prefixed by an 'area-code'. All telephone directories (*guías telefónicas*) show area codes on a map of Spain.

The first coin in the feeder lane drops automatically when connection is made and further coins drop as required. A beep warns the caller when further money is needed to continue the connection. As neither the telephone boxes nor the equipment are sound-proofed, the noise made by falling coins is often enough to interfere with voice reception. It is therefore wise to calculate the charge for the call and then place the highest value coins in the feeder lane so that the intervals between the noise of metal clattering downwards are longer than would be the case with coins of lower denominations.

Telephone boxes do not have their telephone numbers displayed, so one cannot receive incoming calls by pre-arrangement. There is no '999' emergency system but emergency numbers for urgent services are listed in the boxes and in the telephone directories.

Telephone calls cannot be made from post offices.

TELEGRAMS AND CABLES

Telegraph services, which are operated independently of the Post Offices, are usually housed in the same buildings, but their offices often keep different hours. In many large towns, a public telex service is also available at the main post office.

ELECTRICITY

Throughout Spain there is an ample supply of electricity carried by the overhead lines of an extensive grid system linking the hydroelectric and atomic power-stations with cities, towns and villages. Whilst a few parts of the country are still served by 125-volt supplies, most have 220–240 volts, 50 cycles alternating current as in most of Europe, with the 125-volt areas gradually being converted.

Consumer prices are based on the international system of a small standing charge and a further charge per kilowatt-hour consumed, the rate for which diminishes as consumption increases.

When you buy a newly-built property which has not been previously occupied it is the electricity company and not the builder who installs the meter. In this way you are assured of a further professional check on correct and safe installation.

Electrical equipment of all types, made in Spain or imported, is obtainable virtually everywhere.

Electricity companies are regional and it is essential to make contact for meter installation, or for reconnection in the case of a pre-owned house, well in advance of the time it is required. If necessary, the vendor will usually assist a purchaser in approaching the local *Compañia de Electricidad*.

GAS

Except in the large cities, there is no main household gas supply. Some urbanisations have tried installing their own small central supply, but the additional costs make it unattractive to consumers. Most new houses and apartments now have, for heating and cooking, either electricity or stoves which burn the

Public Services and Utilities

ubiquitous bottled butane gas supplied in heavy-duty cylinders of various sizes called '*bombonas*'.

One can buy equipment for virtually every use to which gas can be put; stoves, radiators, lanterns with or without mantles, grills and ovens. There is an initial deposit for the number of cylinders which one calculates will be used per week or month and, from then on, filled cylinders are exchanged for empties as required and only the contents are charged for. Some have capacity gauges incorporated, but if not they can be obtained. Most people rely on experience to judge the frequency of exchange. *Bombonas* can be seen on any day of the week awaiting exchange for filled ones outside houses from the smallest cottage to the largest country villa. Many places have butane delivery services, but in those which do not, one tailors the size or number of one's '*bombonas*' to needs and a car's carrying capacity.

The safety of gas installations is taken very seriously in Spain. All rooms containing equipment for gas for cooking or for water heating are required to have two vents leading outside, one at floor level and another above, for the dispersal of fumes should a leak occur or carbon monoxide be generated. Large cylinders must be kept outside dwellings. Suppliers make spot checks of systems, and pipes that connect gas mains with apparatus are stamped with a date before which they must be renewed.

WATER

Water supplies throughout Spain are generally fairly hard and contain varying amounts of calcium as well as other minerals.

Mains service to private premises is usually metered, with charges calculated per cubic metre (220 Imperial gallons) used, or at a flat rate. Government regulations require public water-supplies to be treated with anti-pollutants. One need have no fear of drinking tap-water as in most places it is perfectly potable especially if one likes a faint taste of chlorine. However, as in most of Europe, except the UK, many people prefer to consume water supplied by one of the many bottling plants which market well or spring water, either flat or with natural or added carbonic gas. The analysis of these waters is shown on the bottle labels. All types are readily available in one- and five-litre bottles, '*con*' (with gas) or '*sin*' (without gas). Many foreigners use the former in place of internationally trade-marked soda waters, which are usually more expensive, as mixers with alcoholic drinks such as brandy or whisky. A term frequently used by English-speaking residents for a whisky and soda is 'Scotch *con gas*'.

All the internationally-marketed soft drinks with brand names such as Coca Cola, Pepsi Cola, Seven-Up, Kas, Schweppes or Finlays Tonic Water are made in Spain under strict quality control and are available almost everywhere.

RUBBISH COLLECTION

Most communities have a large municipal dump area where waste of most types is disposed of, usually by burning.

Collections from private homes and urbanisations are made according to local needs, from daily to twice weekly. This service is paid for, in an organised urbanisation, by its Community Association which reimburses itself for this and other services such as street lighting, by means of annual charges which are usually collected quarterly.

In villas which are not part of an urbanisation, an annual charge is levied by the town council (*Ayuntamiento*) on the registered owner of the dwelling for this service.

MAIL

If it is not delivered, nor collected and then distributed by the management of an urbanisation or apartment complex, mail is obtained by means of a numbered rented mail box at the local post office. There is also a general delivery service, known as '*Lista de Correos*' and to obtain letters addressed care of this, it is necessary to go to the post office armed with your passport for identification.

Outward mail can be posted in any one of the bright scarlet

Public Services and Utilities

and gold painted mail boxes called '*buzones*' located at strategic points in towns and villages.

Most people, however, take their letters to a post office which is open for the same daily period as the banks, obtain the stamps from the counter and use the post-box located in the building. The post office offers surface, air mail and express (or special delivery) as well as registered mail and parcel post services.

Postage stamps are also sold at shops called '*estancos*' whose principal business is the sale of local and foreign manufactured cigarettes and tobaccos and printed Government forms. Except for cigarette machines in some bars and restaurants, '*estancos*' enjoy a virtual monopoly of such sales.

8
Taking up Residence

WHAT TO TAKE

Many people retiring to Spain are not aware that locally manufactured furniture and household equipment of excellent quality and of a variety of price scales are obtainable everywhere. However, there is no reason why you should not import all of your own well-tried and used furnishings and equipment from your home in the UK. It requires a fair amount of planning and paperwork, but there are many removal firms in Britain which offer door-to-door service, taking care of all connected chores.

There is some merit, however, in buying furniture manufactured in Spain because you can make sure that it will fit and match the decor of your new home. By buying electrical or mechanical equipment which, whatever the make, requires servicing from time to time locally, you can obtain after-sales service at reasonable prices or without charge during guarantee periods.

In addition to furniture and household equipment shops, there is no dearth of qualified interior decorators who can plan complete house decoration with great skill and efficiency.

There have been expatriate residents who arrive with little more than the family Bible and photo album and their favourite old gramophone records.

IMPORTING YOUR HOUSEHOLD GOODS

When you establish your permanent residence in Spain you will be able to import your furniture and personal effects, providing they have been in your possession for a minimum of three months, free of customs duties.

Taking up Residence

Import procedures for permanent residence
The following documents should accompany the goods for presentation to the Spanish Customs at the point of entry:

1   An application form, obtainable from the Spanish Consulate general, which requests the Head of Customs Office (*Cambios de Residencia* department) to allow the goods free entry into Spain.
2   This should be accompanied by a list of the items, in Spanish, with the current values of the goods declared in pesetas.
3   Both of the above documents should be signed by you then legalised at the Spanish Consulate General before departure. You will need to make an appointment to do this.
4   It will be necessary to produce your passport when presenting documents at the Consulate General for legalisation.
5   You should provide proof of having obtained Spanish residence. In the event of a residence permit not having been received, you should provide a receipt which states that you have already applied for residence, which you may obtain on application. You may also be required to pay a deposit or produce a bank guarantee at Spanish Customs, which will be returned to you once you have the valid residence permit, and within six months of the importation of the goods.
6   If you are not able to be present to clear Customs when the goods arrive in Spain, your representative should produce a photocopy of the first five pages of your passport. The photocopy should have been previously legalised by the Consulate General.
7   Not all the goods need be imported at the same time as importation may be effected several times within twelve months of your arrival in Spain to take up residence.

Import procedures for a secondary residence
1   The same as in paragraphs 1 to 5 above, except that the application form should be addressed to the head of Customs Office (*Vivienda Segundaria* department).
2   You should provide the Consulate General and the Customs Office with the title deed (*escritura*) of your property in Spain or an agreement to rent a property for a minimum period of

two years. You will be required to provide the Spanish Customs, on entry, with a deposit or a two-year bank guarantee issued by a bank based in Spain, that the goods will remain in the same dwelling, that the property will not be let or sub-let and that it will be reserved for you or your family's exclusive use. As in paragraph 7 above, importation of goods can be effected several times within twelve months.

If you should inherit a Spanish property

The procedures for importing goods are the same as paragraphs 1 to 5 above plus: the production of a notarised death certificate, and the notarised trustee executor's settlement of the estate.

The importation of goods can be effected several times within a period of two years of having taken possession of the inheritance.

WEDDING GIFTS

The same procedure for importation is followed as in paragraphs 1 to 5 above, plus a legalised marriage certificate. In this case the goods may be imported within four months of the wedding ceremony.

See also paragraph 6 above.

PRIVATE MOTOR CARS

If you change your permanent residence from the UK to Spain, you will be able to import your private car free of duty provided that it has been registered in your name for at least six months and used for that period before change of residence. It will be exempt from Spanish Value Added Tax provided that it has been registered in your name for six months before change of residence.

Documentary evidence must be produced that VAT has been paid in the UK. Should the amount be less than that levied in Spain, 33 per cent at the time of writing, the difference will be payable in Spain.

Exemptions are given on condition that the car will not be

sold or transferred before one year has elapsed after the registration of the vehicle in Spain.

Applications for exemption should be addressed to:

Dirección General de Aduanas,
Guzman el Bueno 137,
MADRID 28040.

PETS

To import a pet the following documents must be shown at the Spanish port of entry:
1   A health certificate issued by a veterinary surgeon authorised by the Ministry of Health in the UK, dated no more than 25 days prior to entry.
2   A certificate issued by the Ministry of Agriculture which states that the animal has been kept in an area free of animal diseases and rabies.
Neither of these documents requires legalisation by the Consulate General.

Many foreign residents, like the Spanish, keep cats and dogs and other household pets. There are many breeders of show dogs as well as veterinary clinics where one may apply for and receive, usually in exchange for a small donation to a worthy animal charity, a pick of the strays which are periodically brought in by the local dog catchers. All dogs in Spain must be vaccinated against rabies and wear a collar. A small annual licence is charged. In many towns, the corporation strictly enforces a regulation requiring dogs to be leashed at all times on the public roads.

Whilst you may freely import your pets into Spain, it should be remembered that you will not be able to re-import them into the UK without their undergoing a fairly long period of quarantine. However, there are many boarding kennels which will look after dogs and cats whilst their owners are away.

Living & Retiring in Spain

TAXATION

Any person who spends more than 183 days per year in Spain is considered to be resident and liable for payment of Spanish taxes. However, Britain and Spain have an agreement by which residents may avoid double taxation of income. Her Majesty's Stationery Office, Atlantic House, High Holborn, London, WC1, has published an information leaflet dealing with this agreement. Its title is 'HMSO *Treaty Series 17, 1977*'. It is a 40-page document, and is out of print, but public libraries can usually obtain one for consultation.

The principal taxes in Spain are:

income tax
wealth tax
value added tax
inheritance tax
and, for the property purchaser, *plus valía*

Income tax

The Spanish fiscal year runs from January 1 until December 31.

There are no special tax reliefs for foreign nationals who are Spanish residents.

UK state retirement pensions are paid gross to the recipient wherever resident, and would normally be taxable in the country of residence. Income tax is levied on a person's world-wide income.

Some considerable time after you have been officially resident for more than 183 days you will receive a demand from the local tax collector's office (*Delegación de Hacienda*) which requests details of your and, if married, your spouse's, total income from all sources since you have lived in the country. Capital gains and disposal of assets are included as part of income.

There are several different thresholds and scales and many more deductible items in the income tax system than in Britain. Even for the simplified form which may be used for a return in the case of a very low income, it is essential to consult a tax expert (*asesor fiscal*) of whom there are many with practices in most towns. These professionals will be able to advise you on completing the tax forms (purchased from your local *'estanco'*) and also on obtaining maximum benefit from the Anglo-Spanish Double Taxation Agreement. The consensus amongst Britons who have lived in Spain for many years is that, as a rule, they pay less tax each year than they would were they still resident in the UK.

Wealth tax (*Impuesto sobre el Patrimonio*).

Wealth tax is paid on the value of all of an individual's worldwide property possessed on December 31 each year.

Property means fixed property such as a house and moveable property such as motor cars and personal possessions and investments. For this tax there are also many deductible allowances: recently 9,000,000 pesetas for married couples, plus 750,000 pesetas for each child under 25. It is a small tax which starts at 0.2 per cent for the first 25,000,000 pesetas and usually totals much less than 1 per cent. However, at least until you have been resident for some years, you are best served in all tax matters by consulting an expert.

You purchase both income and wealth tax forms from your local *'estanco'* or tobacconist.

Value Added Tax, VAT (*Impuesto sobre el Valor Añadido* or *IVA*)

On joining the European Economic community Spain instituted *IVA* at rates varying from 6 per cent to 33.3 per cent and abolished the then-current sales taxes. Most of the commodities and services subject to this tax in other EEC countries fall within it. Car hire attracts 12 per cent, and some categories of luxury goods and bills at expensive hotels and restaurants, the maximum rate.

When you purchase new property from a developer it will attract *IVA* at 6 per cent. A pre-owned property purchase is liable to a tax of 5.5 per cent, and this is called transfer tax (*Impuesto de transmisiones*).

Inheritance tax

If a foreign resident legally domiciled there should die in Spain his property would be subject to an inheritance tax, the amount of which would depend on its value at the time and the relationship of those who would benefit. For this reason married couples will often register their property in their joint names. Sometimes, however, registration will be in the names of the children with the parents as life tenants; or in the name of a solely-owned offshore company formed specifically for the purpose. Both these methods can have draw-backs and it is advisable to consult a lawyer and/or tax expert as to the comparative potential advantages.

Plus valía

At the time a property changes hands, local municipalities calculate the increase in the value of the land on which it is built since it was last sold and imposes what is usually a small tax. This is known as the *plus valía* and is collected some time later from the registered owner at that time. If one does not wish to pay the *plus valía* it is necessary to come to an arrangement with the seller whereby the amount is calculated and deducted from the purchase price.

There appears to be no national rate for this tax and it can vary from municipality to municipality.

In cases where a very old property with much surrounding land has not changed hands for many years the *plus valía* could be large and therefore in these cases your lawyer should double-check to ascertain whether there may have been an interim valuation.

Foreign investment paid for by monetary contributions from abroad

If you wished to invest in companies outside Spain whilst you were a resident, using funds from foreign sources, you would not normally require prior authorisation from the Spanish government. However, in some cases previous verification of the projected investment is required by the Department of Foreign

Transactions located in Madrid at: Paseo de la Castellana 167, planta 11 (Madrid). Telephone (91) 259 59 16.

The verification is visualised merely as a control device and approval can be withheld only in exceptional cases where the Spanish authorities consider that the projected investment might give rise to adverse consequences for the country's economy.

The verification is normally completed in less than one month and the investment is tacitly deemed to be approved if no reply is received from the Department of Foreign Transactions within 30 days.

All investments in Spanish companies by foreign residents have to be declared to the foreign investment register of the Department of Foreign Transactions on an easily-completed declaration form.

WILLS

Spanish inheritance laws are very different from those of Britain and there are restrictions on the methods of disposition of a deceased person's property with defined percentages going to surviving spouse and children of the marriage.

There also appears to be some difference of opinion as to which legal system might apply. This is a matter for discussion with your solicitor before you leave and with your Spanish lawyer. It is essential that a will should be made and registered as soon as possible after having obtained a dwelling and residence in Spain.

Advice from your lawyer and local notary should be sought. An 'open' will (*testamento abierto*) will be signed before witnesses and the *notario* and registered in the Central Registry of Wills in Madrid, once a copy has been placed in the *notario's* files. Alternatively, if you want to keep your wishes to yourself, a 'closed' will (*testamento cerrado*) is made by signing it and placing it in an envelope which the notary seals and signs with witnesses before passing it to the Central Registry. Either way you obtain a registration number for future reference.

MEDICAL INSURANCE

Vaccination and inoculation are not required of British subjects visiting Spain from the UK.

Form E111 for short visits, and form E121 for retired persons taking up residence, are obtainable from the DHSS in the UK before departure. These, when presented to the local or provincial capital office of the *Instituto Nacional de la Seguridad Social* (the National Social Security Institute), will entitle you to use the Spanish health service. That office will inform you as to health care and services which are available under Spanish legislation and issue medical identity cards. For any further enquiries you should contact the *Ministerio de Sanidad y Consumo* (Ministry of Health) in Madrid. It is not necessary to pre-register with a doctor.

Foreign residents have access to the many private health insurance companies in Spain which advertise in publications which are in circulation amongst expatriates as well as in the national press. They offer cover for visits to doctors and dentists, most medical fees and hospitalisation. Premiums, of course, can vary according to cover required and are usually paid quarterly.

On effecting a private medical insurance policy a comprehensive booklet which lists names, addresses and telephone numbers of all the general practitioners and specialists connected with the scheme is provided. Clinics and hospitals in each area are also shown.

There are also UK insurance companies which offer coverage for Britons living in or visiting Spain.

HEALTH CARE

There are very few places in Spain without, or not within easy reach of qualified doctors. In many of the popular resorts there are English-speaking physicians and dentists.

As in most countries, some doctors make house calls and others practise only at their offices during specified hours, usually two periods, morning and evening, each day.

Treatment by means of injection is often ordered by doctors

in Spain, but they do not administer it themselves. One goes to a chemist and purchases the prescribed medication and then visits the office of a practising injectionist who is usually a qualified nurse and is known as a *'practicante'* or *'inyeccionista'* who makes the injection and charges a small fee. Many English people dislike treatment by injection and this is well known to Spanish doctors who will often prescribe alternative treatment for British patients.

There are Spanish National Health Service out-patient clinics in most towns and villages.

Chemists

Chemist shops called *'farmacias'* are to be found in every town and village. They operate on a system whereby they take turns to offer 24-hour service, 7 days a week. When closed, all pharmacies display in their window the name and address of the nearest shop offering emergency service. Many chemists in the smaller places live over their shops. Most prescriptions are filled by patent medicines made by Spanish or international pharmaceutical laboratories.

9
Living in Spain

THE CHANGE TO SPAIN

Tourists are said to go to Spain mainly for the sun, which shines at all seasons, and for the miles of Mediterranean and Atlantic beaches. However, for people who retire there it is a complete change of life-style, cuisine, recreation and sporting activities, at a time when they can most enjoy it and, in Spain, can afford it with the added attraction of lower living costs.

As the retirement and tourist regions of Spain have largely been developed, at least initially, by investment from other European countries you will find areas where there are large colonies of people of one nationality: British, Scandinavian, French, German or, in some places, American. But for those who seek the cosmopolitan environment, there are an equal number of places where the foreign population is a mix of residents from many countries. In these you tend to meet more Spaniards, those who live and work there as well as owners of secondary residences. Thus, it is possible to select not only your surroundings, but the type of society in which you will find most interest.

One of the principal changes which will be encountered from the beginning is that to a more outdoor way of life. The patio—in a house, usually a three-sided courtyard in the centre; in an apartment, the terrace or the balcony—will take the place of the drawing room, the dining room or the sitting room in Britain. Although many houses will have these rooms also, it is the patio, with its view of the surrounding country or the sea or the mountains or all three, that becomes the focal point of the family and for guests, for entertainment, and usually most of the meals of the day from breakfast to dinner.

One of the customs which some Britons find strange at first

is the habit of 'dropping in' without notice at almost any time of the day except during the sacrosanct 'siesta hour' in the afternoon. Written or telephoned invitations, several days or more in advance are not the general form in Spain. Spaniards have a saying '*su casa*' (your house), meaning 'you are welcome', when people drop in and this pleasant greeting is soon repeated by new expatriates from more formal countries. Then there is the custom of the regular shaking of hands on encountering friends, and women planting a kiss on each side of the face of others they know well.

The cuisine is completely different from that of northern climes. The Mediterranean diet of mainly fruit, vegetables, fish, chicken, rice and olive oil is somewhat of a change from the food found on the British table: the Sunday roast, ham and eggs or fish and chips. These may be deemed necessary for energy in the commuter world, but a diet lacking animal fat and red meat has served southern European peoples from time immemorial. Besides, the ingredients for such a cuisine are almost always available and because most of them, if not all, can be locally produced in many regions, the cost of items out of season is related to the expense of transport from other areas and not to inflation or import duties in different countries.

There is a wardrobe change as well. Out will go the heavy overcoats, woollen scarves, numerous umbrellas and the green wellies. From mid-April to mid-October or later, women wear summer sports clothes, cotton dresses and lightweight trousers or shorts, whilst for men, short-sleeved shirts and trousers and virtually any sports clothes are the order of the day. Shorts however are seldom seen on male residents in Spain.

From mid-October until April women wear heavier clothes: trousers, skirts and thin sweaters, and men wear sports jackets, slacks, and tweed or flannel suits. All year round, both sexes wear heavy shoes and jeans for the mountain trips often taken on horse or mule.

In Spain the active can remain so, or increase their range of pursuits, while those with other interests have a wide selection of games and hobbies and cultural activities in which to indulge. Your social life can be just what you make it. In most popular retirement areas there is a wide spectrum of social entertainment, from the pre-lunch 'drinkies', to the ever-popular cocktail party, and the more formal wining and dining.

There are societies of all kinds, national groupings (there are several British societies in different regions), there are gatherings of many sorts from garden to bridge clubs and, of course, all sports from golf and tennis to clay pigeon shooting and fishing, which have regular get-togethers.

One custom that often confuses British residents when they first move to Spain is that of Spanish women retaining their maiden names after marriage so that often, when you are introduced at a party, unless a couple are together, you may have no indication as to the name of the husband.

SHOPPING

Most of the international brand-name canned or frozen foods and many of the drinks that one finds on the counters of Europe and America are available, made in Spain. Their manufacture, either in branch-factories or under licence, is subject to the same quality control as in their countries of origin with the result that, apart from the labels, which in order to comply with strict government requirements often include fuller details of ingredients than is demanded elsewhere, it is virtually impossible to differentiate between the original and the Iberian product.

In all the large towns are modern self-service supermarkets carrying a very wide variety of foods as well as many other goods. They are generally open until late in the evening six days a week although most close for the habitual siesta hours. In addition, there are numerous small shops announcing variously '*Alimentación*', '*Comestibles*' or '*Ultramarinos*' or sometimes simply '*Super*' where one can obtain practically all one needs in tins or in the form of packed and unpacked foods, fresh meat, vegetables, fruit, fish, cheese and garnishings, together with soft drinks, wines and spirits.

One can seldom do better in terms of freshness, price and quality than in the municipal markets. These spacious, clean, local-government-controlled food outlets are found in every town and in many of the larger villages. They are also centres for the exchange of news and gossip, not only for Spaniards but also for foreign residents and vacationers.

In large resort areas, some foreigners, following the example of many Spaniards, drive into the nearby countryside to shop where prices can be better than in markets which have to cater for seasonal tourist demand fluctuations.

Shopping in the smaller retail outlets becomes a pleasant pastime because of the polite and cheerful manner of the salespeople and the personal touch that is often lost in the mechanised purchasing centres of metropolitan areas. One soon learns that the freely-offered advice as to what one should or should not buy is well worth accepting for what it is: the friendly gesture of experts towards people who are guests in their midst.

In addition to the municipal and supermarkets and small shops, some areas, especially ones more remote from the large villages and towns, are served by *'ventas ambulantes'*. These are vans of various sizes fitted out as small shops which travel around the countryside selling virtually anything which is required for the care and feeding of the average household.

For those who hanker after more mundane forms of retail commerce, many cities have branches of the large Madrid and Barcelona department stores and such international emporiums as Woolworth, and in some areas Colonel Sanders competes for business with Wimpy and Pam-Pam.

Prices can vary from town to town and often from shop to shop in each, by as much as 10 per cent from one side of the street to the other. It is usually worth while for the economy-minded to look around and compare prices. Many commodities have their prices clearly printed on the package preceded by the letters *'PVP'*, an abbreviation of *'Precio de Venta al Público'* (price for sale to the public).

One of the many advantages of residence in Spain is that one can obtain fresh food, especially salads and fruits, practically throughout the year. Lettuce, cucumbers, onions and many varieties of beans are almost always in season. Now that tomatoes are grown under plastic for quick ripening purposes and to protect them from lower temperatures and windburn in the winter months, several crops are harvested each year. Fruit of one variety or another is usually available but there can be a dearth of good citrus fruit between June and November. Strawberries, pears, apples, peaches, apricots, grapes and cherries and most other temperate as well as some tropical fruit such as *chirimoya* (custard apple) and avocado pears, can all be obtained in their seasons.

One rule of thumb for economical shopping is to look for goods grown or produced nearby, when the transport element in their selling price will be much smaller. Buy local products whenever possible.

Municipal markets have fresh and frozen fish sections stocking locally-caught and Atlantic fish brought in by a lorry from Cantabria. Most supermarkets stock frozen fish as well as the popular dried variety known as *bacalao* or salt cod.

Wood for fires

Often houses and apartments have open fireplaces and many varieties of wood are available as fuel. Should there be a winter cold snap, salesmen in trucks will tour towns and villages offering off-cuts from sawmills, waste from construction projects, and logs and roots from old olive trees. Olive wood provides by far the greatest heat but takes a long time to ignite. For those who like the illusion of a cold northern winter in a land of warm sun, a roaring fire, especially at Christmas time, can be effective. Coal and charcoal can be obtained but are not widely available.

HOUSEHOLD HELP

In or near towns and villages, household help can be obtained fairly easily, but one must usually count on having to provide transport to and fro.

Costs for daily or live-in help—the latter are not as available as the former—are low relative to some other European countries and vary according to area. Gardeners are also available in most places on an hourly, daily, or more permanent basis.

Social security is paid by employers for servants or other

domestic employees who work for more than 18 hours in a week.

A unique facet of the Spanish system is that all such workers are entitled to receive an extra month's wage in July and again in December. According to how you look at it, this arrangement is either an imposition or can be welcomed as a means of ensuring a lasting relationship with a good employee.

There are dry-cleaning establishments as well as self-service launderettes in all but the smallest towns. Commercial laundries operate in the cities.

Residence for a short time in a community, small or large, enables you to locate the many small businesses that will undertake, at short notice, such chores as fixing a plumbing fault, cleaning the filter of a washing-machine or checking electrical equipment. Often they will also rent out pieces of gardening or other equipment which you might need for a short period only. It is largely a question of getting to know the side-streets of your area.

10
Leisure Pursuits

INLAND TRANSPORTATION

Air
Iberia and its associated airlines connect all the major cities, the Balearics, Melilla and the Canaries, with Madrid and with each other by scheduled flights.

Railways
From Madrid, which is located at almost the exact centre of the country, RENFE, the State railway company, connects all Spain with all Europe from two major stations.

Bus services
RENFE also operates special express road services between Madrid and a number of the principal resort cities using 50-seat air-conditioned double-decker buses with toilets, colour video screen, individual reading lights and, as well as a small 16-seat cafe-restaurant on the lower deck, hot and cold drink machines and a hostess. These fast services connect the capital with Málaga, Marbella, Alicante, Murcia, La Manga, Badajoz, and San Sebastián, amongst others.

In addition to the special services of RENFE, most of Spain is connected by modern buses running to timetables of which copies are obtainable at the bus stations. Many of these bus stations offer bar and restaurant services for travellers. On some routes tickets are purchased on boarding.

Taxis

Virtually all towns and villages offer taxi-services, in the larger conurbations from stands in or near shopping centres. For local journeys most cabs are metered, whilst for longer trips one should consult the driver in advance as to the charge. Taxis carry up to five adults and the fares charged are for the cab, not per passenger. There are fixed prices for long journeys and for railway station and airport services.

BY CAR

Retirement is often a time when you invest in a new car. You have probably, in the past, owned or been supplied with a vehicle, possibly too large for economical everyday life when business travel ceases and your main outdoor activities are shopping, visiting and the golf club. However, when you become resident in Spain you will no doubt wish, as do most people, to take full advantage of the touring opportunities offered by the vast and interesting Iberian Peninsula, and a car selected for your changed environment and needs is required.

Spain has some of the finest engineered and built motorways in Europe, in a network continually under expansion. It also has hundreds of miles of rough-surfaced minor roads that lead to beauty spots, historic monuments and other evidence of its fascinating past. It has roads that follow the coastline and roads that climb up to and pass through high mountain areas of which the Pyrenees, the Sierra Guadarrama and the Sierra Nevada are but a few.

The ideal car for use in Spain is one which is not too wide nor too long, which has a tough suspension system and is relatively economical. It should have plenty of room for shopping and picnic equipment, be reliable and comfortable whether at speed on a four-lane motorway or climbing the narrow rough route to the Sierra Nevada from the south, one of the highest roads in Europe.

Most car manufacturers produce suitable vehicles and on taking up residence you may import your car from Britain without paying import duty, providing you have owned it for a minimum of 6 months (see p. 60; Private Motor Cars). A vehicle with left-hand steering is essential for safety, but this is not easily obtained from stock in the UK and usually requires special pre-ordering.

Spain has its own considerable motor car industry and manufactures various models of Seat (now no longer part-owned by Fiat), Peugeot-Citroën, Renault, Ford and General Motors. Prices, of course, vary according to model, but in general are said to be comparable with those of the same types in other European countries, allowing for the exchange factor.

No annual Ministry of Transport inspection certificate is required in Spain. Third party insurance called obligatory cover (*seguro obligatorio*) is compulsory, and must be taken out with a Spanish company. There are annual road taxes based on the size of the engine.

If you should take your Spanish-registered car to the UK it need not be declared at Customs if you are not staying longer than 6 months, which presumably you would not wish in view of UK tax liability.

MOTORING

If you visit Spain to select the place and house in which you will take up residence on retirement, you will be able to drive your own or a rented car on your British driving licence supported by an International Driving Permit, obtainable at the time of writing at the Royal Automobile Club or the Automobile Association, at a cost of £2. When you become a permanent resident you exchange your British licence for one issued by the local Traffic Department in the area where you live. You will not have to pass a driving test, but you will be required to present your passport, your residence permit and three photographs. Your Spanish licence will normally be valid for the period and vehicles covered by your British licence. However, when you are required to renew it you may have to present a certificate from your doctor and, of course, more photographs. The effortless way to deal with your licence requirements is to let your local *Gestoria* handle them.

Traffic in Spain proceeds on the right-hand side of the road and standard European traffic signs are used.

Speed limits are: a maximum of 120 kilometres per hour (75 m.p.h.) on motorways, 100 k.p.h. (62 m.p.h.) on main roads and 90 k.p.h. (55 m.p.h.) and lower where marked, on other roads. If you tow a caravan or a trailer of any size you are limited to a maximum of 80 k.p.h. (50 m.p.h.) on motorways and 70 k.p.h. (43 m.p.h.) on all other roads.

Road discipline is maintained by the highway section of the *Guardia Civil*, known as '*tráficos*', in cars or more often in pairs on motorcycles. They can often be seen standing, one at each side of the road, in places where long wide stretches might encourage high speeds, or at double-white-lined hill crests or blind corners, to deter the incautious from attempting to overtake.

Radar and other speed enforcement measures are often used including sometimes the taking of a photographic record of your number-plate as you pass. You receive your speeding ticket by mail some time later.

You are required to signal not only when moving out of lane to pass, but also when returning to lane.

The use of front-seat seat-belts is obligatory on all inter-urban journeys. Children under ten years of age are not permitted to travel in the front seats of cars. All vehicles are required to carry a spare set of light bulbs as well as a warning triangle for use in the event of a breakdown, in addition to hazard lights, if fitted.

The offices of the Royal Automobile Club of Spain are always most helpful to visting motorists whether or not they are members of a similar organisation in their own country.

You should always carry, in addition to your passport, your driving permit, your car registration papers and insurance certificates and the bail bond suggested by the motoring associations in Britain.

Lorry traffic of all kinds is very heavy on main roads at most hours of the day and night. The drivers are invariably remarkably courteous. They usually signal following traffic with their direction indicators when it is dangerous to pass. At night, most trucks are festooned with lights that indicate the full extent of the vehicle.

On steep parts of inter-provincial main roads, compulsory slow traffic lanes are located at strategic intervals on hills to allow faster vehicles to overtake lorries with safety.

On long journeys, especially in the heat of summer, many motorists take a very early (by Spanish standards) picnic lunch and then drive during the conventional lunch and siesta period when many trucks, and much other traffic, are off the road.

Service stations are abundant on main roads and many are open 24 hours. They sell 92 octane (*normal* or *gasolina*) and 97 octane (*super*) petrol, and all carry diesel fuel which is priced less than petrol. A long-established custom is to offer a small tip to petrol-station attendants for filling your tank, especially as they will generally check your oil and wipe your front and rear windscreens.

Dipped headlights are required on all roads as soon as the twilight period ends, during which side-lights are acceptable. As elsewhere, one must always dip headlights in the face of approaching traffic.

The use of dipped headlights is obligatory in tunnels, many of which are unlit.

Oil changing and maintenance should be carried out with greater frequency in Spain than in colder countries, as exposure to dust, salt-laden sea air and heat tends to increase the deterioration rate of car engines and bodies.

Automatic car-washes outside the main cities and towns are relatively scarce, but most rural petrol stations will arrange for a car to be hand-washed and polished on request.

TOURING FROM YOUR SPANISH HOME

Many Britons choose Spain as a place for retirement because of the potential for the enjoyment of leisurely peregrination by car or bus or ship.

After the overcrowded motorways and main roads of much of Britain the highways and byways of the Iberian Peninsula make motoring one of the pleasures for which the automobile must have been invented.

From any part of southern Spain there are superb main and secondary roads linking yesterday with today, historic cities with ultra-modern holiday playgrounds. Except in the high vacation seasons, these roads are never overburdened with traffic, petrol is usually available day or night, and you will find hostelries and restaurants to suit every pocket, which are open for so long each day that you can be sure of finding a meal at any time or a place to sleep without prior reservation.

The Spanish National Tourist Offices publish a number of superb pocket geographic and historical guides to many parts of the country away from the popular tourist beaches.

The 'Route of the White Towns', about 335 km (210 miles), takes you through places of natural grandeur, with historic monuments and relics of many civilisations. The route passes Tarifa, the southernmost town in Europe, and Cape Trafalgar, through Ronda, founded by the Romans and one of the oldest towns in Spain, with a three-arched bridge carrying the road 90 m (295 ft) above the gorge which divides the town; via twenty or more towns, all with houses painted white to deflect the heat of the summer sun. A day, a week or a month can be taken for a tour such as this.

For admirers of the works of Cervantes, a visit to La Mancha, the central plateau of Spain, the region of the adventures of the intrepid Don Quixote, with his faithful servant Sancho Panza, is detailed in another publication of the department of tourism. According to where you live, this tour, which covers a large area of the central plateau, can be commenced from a number of places: Albacete, Cuenca, Ciudad Real or Toledo. It is probably best to go first to Madrid, and combine it with a visit to the capital and from there head for Toledo, just 40 miles to the south. Madrid is 392 miles from Barcelona (Costa Brava), 217 miles from Valencia (Costa del Azahar), 260 miles from Alicante (Costa Blanca), 345 miles from Málaga (Costa del Sol) and 660 miles from Cádiz (Costa de la Luz). Even with the vast sections of superb highway along the routes it is a good day's drive from most places.

In addition to over 70 National Tourist *paradors* (excellent 3- and 4-star hotels strategically located throughout Spain for tourists' use) there is also a great variety of hotels and inns of all categories, whilst in many places off the beaten track small bar-restaurants will often offer simple accommodation for travellers.

In the winter sports seasons in the resorts of the Pyrenees and the Sierra Nevada there is good skiing within easy reach of residents of the Costa Brava and the coastal areas of Granada and Málaga. Many from Catalonia visit the small Pyrenean State of Andorra for the same reasons.

Mediterranean and Atlantic cruising as well as visits to Tangier, Fez, Casablanca, Marrakesh and other northern Moroccan cities and the Atlas Mountains, are all within reach of residents of southern Spain. Travel agents in each coastal area offer package tours by air, coach and boat, to other Spanish regions and to Morocco and Gibraltar.

For land touring you should obtain a list of national and local fiestas, published annually by the tourism authorities, and plan your land tours so that your visits will coincide with celebrations that interest you.

RESTAURANTS

Spanish restaurants, in most places, offer regional as well as national or international cuisine. Restaurants to suit virtually every taste and pocket are found throughout the country. Many bars, especially on the inter-provincial main roads, also serve limited menu meals.

Dining hours are probably the latest in Europe and 9 pm is likely to be considered early for an evening meal, whilst lunch times can stretch from 2 pm until 4.30 pm and later.

Every restaurant and bar-restaurant is obliged to offer and display a table d'hôte fixed-price menu of a small number of courses at a minimum price (according to the number of forks from one to four, the means by which the status of an eating place is officially classified) and including bread and a small quantity of house wine, beer or mineral water. In the resorts these menus are frequently listed as *'menus turísticos'* (tourist menus).

In bar-restaurants, the prices of drinks and meals vary according to where you consume them. Cheapest is at the counter, standing, or sometimes in better-class bars, sitting on stools; more expensive is at a table where you are served by a waiter; and if there is an outside terrace, there is a still higher charge for service there.

Restaurant and bar prices always include a charge for service, but it is customary to leave some small change for the waiter for good service.

TAPAS BARS

In every town and village in Spain one finds what are known as *'tapas* bars'. *'Tapa'* is the Spanish word for a lid or cover. At one time, open air bars served small pieces of bread which customers placed over their drinks between sips to protect them from dust and the heat of the sun. Gradually, the *tapas* became small fish or meat snacks, grew larger, and were no longer offered free of charge. Today, many *tapas* bars, especially in the larger towns, resemble delicatessens and offer an enormous variety of hors-d'oeuvres, both hot and cold.

PENSIONERS' CLUBS (*Hogares de Pensionistas*)

In most Spanish towns and some of the larger villages, one will find an *'Hogar de Pensionistas'* or pensioners' club, operated under the aegis of the Ministry of Health and Social Security.

The club is usually situated in a centrally-located building and is well furnished with leather armchairs which would do credit to a London club. It has a bar with coffee service, television, local newspapers and other amenities, and some enjoy occasional attendance by a local doctor for minor ailments of members.

Whilst membership is primarily Spanish, such is Spanish egalitarian hospitality that any person over 65, or who can show that he or she is a pensioner, qualifies and foreign residents are welcomed.

Members obtain their drinks and coffees at prices slightly lower than in commercial establishments.

Pensioners are also able to travel on the Spanish government railways at a considerably reduced fare on designated days, on production of identification.

Many British and other northern Europeans residing in Spain take full advantage of pensioners' privileges.

GOLF

The climate of southern Spain makes it possible for the golf enthusiast to play almost any day of the year. Virtually all of the popular resort and retirement areas have, within easy reach, 9, 18 or 36 hole golf courses, most with club houses and amenities. Generally, they are operated as private clubs, some with affiliation to clubs in Britain or other European countries.

Their number is constantly increasing as the popularity of Spain for retirement and holidays grows, and there must be well over a hundred superb courses throughout the country with some 40 of them along the south and south-western coasts. Some of them have been designed by such international experts as Robert Trent Jones. Usually there are cart-hire facilities. Below is a list of some of the best known golf courses.

Andalusia
Club de Campo de Málaga, 18 holes par 72. Near the city of MÁLAGA
Atalaya Golf and Country Club, 18 holes par 72. MARBELLA, Málaga
Club de Golf de Mijas, 18 holes par 72. FUENGIROLA, Málaga
Golf Guadalmina, 36 holes par 72. SAN PEDRO DE ALCÁNTARA, Malaga
Club de Golf Nerja, 9 holes par 58. NERJA, Málaga
Golf El Paraiso, 18 holes par 72. ESTEPONA, Málaga
Club de Golf Las Brisas, 18 holes par 72. MARBELLA, Málaga

Club de Golf Valderrama, 18 holes par 72. SOTOGRANDE,
   Cádiz
Club de Golf Sotogrande, 18 holes par 72. SOTOGRANDE,
   Cádiz
Golf San Andres, 9 holes par 36. CHICLANA, Cádiz
Club de Golf Bellavista, 9 holes 72. HUELVA, Huelva
Golf Almerimar, 18 holes par 72. EJIDO, Almería
Cortijo Grande Club de Golf, 18 holes par 70. TURRE, Almería
Club Playa Granada, 9 holes par 70. MOTRIL, Granada

Costa Brava

Real Club de Golf El Prat, 27 holes par 72. 17 kilometres from
   BARCELONA
Club de Golf Vallromanas, 18 holes par 72. VALLROMANAS,
   Barcelona
Barcelona Club de Golf Costa Brava, 18 holes par 70. SANTA
   CRISTINA DE ARO,

Gerona

Club de Golf Terramar, 18 holes par 70. SITGES, Barcelona

Costa Dorada

Club de Golf Costa Dorada, 9 holes par 72. TARRAGONA,
   Tarragona

Costa de Azahar

Club de Golf Costa de Azahar, 9 holes par 66. CASTELLÓN,
   Castellón

Costa Blanca

La Manga Campo de Golf, 18 holes par par 71. LOS BELONES,
   Cartagena
Club de Campo El Bosque, 18 holes par 72. CHIVA, Valencia
Club de Golf Ifach, 9 holes par 30. BENISA, Alicante

HUNTING, SHOOTING AND FISHING

In order to import firearms a certificate will have to be obtained from the Spanish Consulate General. For this production of a valid British firearms licence plus a photocopy for retention is required.

On arrival in Spain you present the Consular certificate to the relevant authorities, and it will be exchanged for the appropriate Spanish licence.

There are two kinds of land on which you may hunt or shoot: those of common use and those of special administration, that is to say national reserves, national parks, and private shooting lands, the last usually marked by small white metal triangles on a black background placed at the boundaries of the preserves and sometimes with a printed sign '*coto privado*' (private estate).

Once you have obtained a hunting licence you may hunt freely in open seasons on all lands of common use. To hunt on land under special administration, you require permission from the title-holders, whether they be private or official.

To hunt on national reserves, a special government permit must be obtained which depends, among other things, on the species of animal to be hunted.

Big game hunting

Big game hunting in Spain is for stag, buck, roebuck, ibex, several species of wild goat, wild boar, wolf, lynx and bear. The last two enjoy special protection. Open seasons and types of weapon which may be used are controlled by the Ministry of Agriculture. There are companies which organise hunting expeditions.

Small game hunting or shooting

Shooting, in the open seasons, is usually for grouse, waterfowl, partridge, turtle-dove, dove and the bustard, a terrestrial bird related to the crane. There are a number of companies which specialise in organising shoots. The Spanish Tourist Office, 57/58 St James's Street, London, SW1 will supply names and addresses of those which operate in the areas in which you wish to hunt or shoot. These companies will obtain for clients the necessary licences and the obligatory insurance cover.

Fishing

There is every type of fishing available in Spain in mountain streams, rivers, lakes, reservoirs and from the beaches and deep sea fishing in the Mediterranean and the Atlantic. There are two types of inland waters, those which are subject to general regulations and those which are reserves or privately owned. To fish the last two of these, permission must be obtained from the owners or from the National Institute for the Conservation of Nature (*ICONA*) with offices in most provincial capitals.

Some of the many species of fish found in Spanish waters are salmon, trout, the common and royal carp, pickerel or pike, black bass, mullet, tuna, bonito, swordfish and shark. There are defined open and closed seasons for fishing, limitations on the size and numbers of catch of certain fish and hours for fishing. Licences are required and obtained from *ICONA* or from the provincial tourist offices, which also issue fishing guides for the serious fisherman with extensive information for each area.

SAILING

Sailing is a very popular sport for Spaniards, residents and tourists. There are yacht clubs and marinas in many of the popular resorts and in the harbours of cities, towns and villages. Boats of almost every type from the humble dinghy to the large motor yacht can be seen in Spanish waters, especially in the summer. Bare-boat rental (without crew) is possible in most beach areas. It is a popular pastime for residents to use small inflatable boats with outboard motors to reach the hundreds of small coves along the Mediterranean coastline often difficult to reach by land, for picnics and bathing.

TENNIS

Amongst Spaniards, permanent foreign residents and tourists, tennis is possibly the favourite form of recreation and is played virtually all year round.

There are courts, private and public, in the gardens of the large and often even the smallest hotels, and in the grounds surrounding the large developments, many of them available for a small subscription to non-residents. Many of the larger villas boast private courts. It would be hard for the tennis enthusiast not to be able to arrange a game at almost any time.

Tennis equipment is available everywhere and the dress of players can vary from just shorts and tops in the summer months, to the one time *de rigueur* Wimbledon apparel in the cooler days. In the very long summer evenings the game is played until late and, often, if the weather is particularly hot, under sodium lighting after darkness falls. Most courts are hard and usually coloured, with green centres and red surrounds or vice versa.

ON THE BEACH

Even if you live some way inland you will find that you will spend much time at the beach. There you will find that, in addition to swimming, it is possible to hire beach equipment, wind surf boards, motor or sail boats, water-skis or scuba masks, from organised licensed pitches.

Resort beaches in Spain differ from those in many other countries, where the sand stretches are reserved for relaxing or sports activities and where cafés, bars, boutiques, ice-cream stands, restaurants and snack-bars are located along the peripherals. Perhaps because of the busy main roads which, in many cases, hug the coastline, such amenities, especially the last two, are often located on the beach itself. Some of the longer, wider and more popular beaches may have as many as half a dozen snack-bars or restaurants open from dawn to sunset and, in keeping with Spanish eating habits, in summer until much later. It is thus often possible to spend the whole day and much of the night at the beach with every requirement close at hand.

11
Cultural Life

THEATRE

Spain numbers two Nobel prize-winners amongst its many dramatists—Benavente and Echegaray—and the Spanish theatre, both classical and modern, is of international importance.

There are touring companies who present Spanish and foreign plays and *Zarzuela*, a Spanish form of light opera, in the theatres of all the major cities. There are regular festivals of Latin and Greek drama in Mérida; of Spanish classical drama in Almagro, Ciudad Real; and of avant-garde theatre in Sitges near Barcelona.

In some of the resorts with a large number of English-speaking permanent residents there are local amateur companies who play at theatres and hotels, offering English and American works.

Flamenco, the ebullient Spanish gypsy music, is played—or perhaps 'performed' is a better word—at theatres, night-clubs, on the beaches and in the streets at fiestas throughout Spain, especially in Andalusia.

CINEMA

In spite of the growth of television, the cinema is still a major form of entertainment in Spain and there are a great number of cinemas throughout the country with daily shows and weekly or twice-weekly changes of programme. There is a wide distribution system for films, and major pictures are often released as quickly as in New York, London or Paris. 'The night out at the cinema' has not lost popularity amongst the young or old.

Most pictures, if not made in Spanish, are dubbed but there are clubs where English versions of major films can be seen, especially in hotels and some urbanisations, since the introduction of direct satellite broadcast reception.

FIESTAS

There are fiestas or festivals throughout Spain all the year round. Some are traditional, dating back to the middle ages and beyond and others, such as the International Film Festival held each year in San Sebastián are very much of the twentieth century. Most are of religious origin whether they be the Magdalene Festivals at Castellón de la Plana or the celebrations that take place in almost every town and village on the birthday of the local community's patron Saint. Then there are festivals in honour of the fruits of the land such as the Rice Festival and the Wine Harvest Festival in the province of Valencia, the Saffron Rose Festival in Toledo and the Exaltation of Shellfish in El Grove in Pontevedra. The two most religious festivals are perhaps those of Holy Week in Seville and Corpus Christi in Toledo.

Whatever their origin, Spanish festivals are full of music, colour, excitement and religious fervour.

There are a number of international music festivals such as a week of chamber music in Segovia and an international jazz festival in San Sebastián, most of them taking place annually.

MUSEUMS

The most famous of Spain's many museums is the art gallery; the Prado in Madrid, where the works of some of her greatest artists, Velázquez, Goya, El Greco, Ribera, Zurbarán and Murillo, are on display alongside Flemish primitives and Italian renaissance painters.

The art of north-eastern Spain is on view at the Museum of Catalonian Art in Barcelona, where there is also the Picasso Museum. The National Archaeological Museum in Madrid has a large important collection of coins and pottery and in the museums of many provincial capitals can be found examples of ancient, modern and contemporary art.

Cultural Life

LOCAL ART

Over recent years southern Spain has developed a number of centres for the arts and has attracted as residents artists, writers and photographers, amateur and professional, from many countries. They can often be seen at work on the beaches, in the mountains and in the cafes. In some towns the local branches of the major banks offer the walls of their outer public offices for the display of the work of resident craftsmen. Thus, especially in winter, in the larger resorts there are art exhibitions almost every week.

RELIGIOUS SERVICES

There are churches ministering to the Roman Catholic faith in all towns and villages throughout Spain. Times of Masses are frequently posted on small signs strategically located at the main road entrances to centres of population as well as outside the churches.

Spain is in the Anglican Diocese of the Bishop of Gibraltar in Europe, The Right Reverend John R. Satterthwaite at the time of writing. There are churches named after England's patron Saint George in Madrid, Barcelona and Málaga. There are resident Anglican clergy in a number of tourist and retirement areas:

In Altea (Alicante) the Rev. A. V. Albutt for Benidorm, Calpe, Altea, Campello, Jávea, Denia and Moraira.
(Times and places of services are published in the *Costa Blanca News*.)
In Fuengirola (Málaga) the Rev. R. S. Matheson for Benalmádena Costa, Fuengirola, Torremolinos, Calahonda, Mijas and Chiclana de la Frontera (Cádiz).
In San Pedro de Alcántara (Málaga) the Rev. W. B. Vane, for Estepona, Algeciras (Cádiz) and Sotogrande (Cádiz).
In Frigiliana (Málaga) the Rev. D. Cherry for Málaga, Nerja and Almuñecar (Granada).
(*SUR*, an English-language weekly published in Málaga, lists details of services.)

Anglican services are often conducted in premises borrowed from other denominations or in schools or church halls.

There are synagogues in a number of municipalities.

RADIO AND TELEVISION

Spain is served by a network of government radio stations as well as, in some places, commercial stations, broadcasting on the medium and long wave bands for about 18 hours each day, with many transmitting also on the FM/VHF bands. A wide variety of programmes is offered, interspersed with newscasts and commentaries. Some, especially FM/VHF stations, broadcast principally classical music, opera light and heavy, *zarzuela* (Spanish operetta) and news throughout the day. Such international events as the Salzburg Festival are often broadcast live by relay arrangements with European services.

Spanish television programmes broadcast in colour using the PAL system or in black and white on the Norma G. can be received throughout the country. On frequent occasions during the year, Eurovision programmes are broadcast, especially football matches and other sporting events of international interest. In Andalusia, some Moroccan stations can be received as the transmitting system used in that country is the same as in Spain. At the south-western end of the province of Málaga both radio and television English-language broadcasts from Gibraltar can be received on British or double-standard sets.

British and American television sets made for SECAM reception requires modification for use in Spain.

World-wide television

In 1985 direct broadcast reception from satellites became available in Spain. A number of hotels and urbanisations installed dishes to receive the signals which may then be distributed to individual sets. Similar dishes were installed in the gardens or on the roofs of private villas and houses. Thus, according to the diameter of the 'dish', viewers can watch programmes broadcast from virtually any country in the world where signals are transmitted via satellite. The number of such 'dishes' is rapidly

Cultural Life

increasing and full installation and maintenance services are available in the major areas.

There is no licensing system in Spain for the use of radio and television sets.

English-language radio programmes from abroad

The World Service programmes of the BBC are beamed so as to cover the Iberian Peninsula during much of the 24 hours. Transmissions are sufficiently powerful to enable them to be received on the simpler sets.

'Voice of America' short-wave English-language programmes can be heard as well as some of the American Forces stations in northern Europe, similarly Canadian Broadcasting Corporation and Canadian Forces transmissions can be heard.

For a small annual fee, the BBC will mail to individuals details of their overseas programmes and current wavelengths in the form of an attractive monthly illustrated magazine entitled *London Calling*.

NEWSPAPERS, MAGAZINES AND BOOKS

In addition to regional newspapers, most Madrid daily papers are on sale throughout Spain. Popular and quality papers from the major European capitals are available in the resort areas and many provincial cities on the day of publication.

UK daily papers are obtainable on the same day, as are British Sunday papers which, however, are usually sold without their colour magazines. Some American daily papers such as the *New York Times* and the *Wall Street Journal* are carried by major newsagents usually two or three days old and the *New York Herald Tribune*, printed in London and Paris, on the publication day.

Prices of all foreign publications are invariably higher than in their countries of origin, for obvious reasons. Most newspapers and many magazines carry their peseta price on the front page or cover.

Many newspapers offer airmail subscriptions at advantageous prices, but it is seldom that you will receive these by mail on the day of publication. There is a similar problem with weekly and monthly magazines, although you usually obtain them before the publication at source of the succeeding edition.

Bookstalls carry many news-magazines such as *The Economist, Newsweek, Time, Le Point, Der Spiegel* and so on, although usually a little after publication date.

Some resort areas are served by English-language weeklies published *in situ*. The best known of these is perhaps *SUR* in English, published in Málaga which circulates throughout Andalusia, as does the glossy English-language monthly magazine, the long established *Lookout*, also published in Málaga. In Alicante there is the *Costa Blanca Post*; in Almería *The Entertainer*; in Nerja (Málaga) the *New Panorama* and in Madrid the *Iberian Sun*.

Books

Fiction and non-fiction books in many languages, hardback and paperback, are on sale everywhere. English-language bestsellers appear soon after publication. There are also many small lending libraries, usually operated by foreign residents, which offer paperbacks in English and other languages on a sale and guaranteed re-purchase basis.

Books dealing with Spanish history, culture, art, music, letters, sports and politics are on sale in many languages, although the last-named are seldom in translation.

There are guidebooks to the whole of the Iberian Peninsula, area by area, the majority profusely illustrated with colour photographs and maps, as well as a plethora of Spanish and foreign publications for the study of the Spanish language.

There is really no reason for the person wishing to retire to Spain to relax and catch up with all the reading for which he or she has never been able to find time, to bring his or her library to Spain. He or she will find anything which is required either immediately at hand or easily obtainable.

Cultural Life

LEARNING THE LANGUAGE

In almost every large town there are facilities for foreigners to learn Spanish, either at language schools or with private teachers. Many Spanish universities offer special summer courses for foreigners and one- or two-year courses for those who wish to become highly proficient in this beautiful and expressive language.

There is no reason why the average person retiring to Spain should not be able to read the local newspapers and converse with Spanish friends within a relatively short time.

12
Leaving Your Spanish Home

PREPARING FOR AN EXTENDED ABSENCE

Burglary and housebreaking are increasing in most parts of Europe, and Spain is no exception. It behoves owners who leave their houses unoccupied for extended periods to take precautions to protect the contents in their absence.

Whilst many villas and apartments have wrought-iron bars over windows and similarly constructed outer doors to enable free air to circulate whilst maintaining privacy, and others use roller or sliding shutters for the same reason, such protection for a vacant dwelling will deter only the amateur or sneak-thief.

Theft insurance of all types is available, usually at reasonable rates, but one should read the small print on the policies very carefully. For instance some companies require an uninhabited property to be checked at regular, usually short, intervals by someone who has the confidence of the owner, in order to maintain cover. Policies which do not contain this proviso are frequently expensive. Policies of the major companies often carry an official English translation printed under each line.

After insuring one's property and its contents, it is usual to take a few extra precautions to deter thieves and make it as difficult as possible for them to enter and remove your goods.

General insurance

Virtually anything which can be insured in Britain, from houses to boats, and furniture to paintings, can be covered by the policies offered by the local agents of the major Spanish and

British insurance companies, most of whom advertise in the daily press or in foreign-language publications.

CARE OF YOUR PROPERTY DURING YOUR ABSENCE

In addition to insurance of your property and its contents against theft and fire, there are other precautions which can be taken to maintain your home in first-class condition.

In many towns and resorts there are people, many of them English-speaking, who are engaged in the business of looking after houses and apartments whilst the owners are not in residence. They inspect each property on a regular basis, open windows for an hour or so on each visit to ventilate the rooms, check the plumbing for traces of leaks and arrange for repairs under their supervision. They flush lavatories to ensure that no water-breeding insects have a chance to propagate and, should there have been a storm, survey the roof for signs of loose tiles, or obtain a gardener to tidy the flower-beds and mow the lawn so that you do not return to a delightful wilderness.

If left funds they will attend to the payment of water, electricity and tax bills which might arrive at the owner's post office box in his absence, and will clean and provision the dwelling prior to his return. For these services they charge a pre-arranged monthly fee commensurate with the value of the property.

Such people are considered to be self-employed and are often retired British couples who bolster their pensions by carrying out these jobs. They usually advertise by placing cards on the notice-boards which can be found in most bars and small restaurants popular with expatriates.

13
Working in Spain

Spain is a member of the European Economic Community, but it will be some years before clauses of the Treaty of Rome referring to the free movement of workers within the Community take effect. In the meantime, to work for an employer in Spain, it is necessary for a national of an EEC country to obtain a work permit.

It is, however, unlikely that a permit to take up paid employment would be issued to a person over retirement age.

As a general rule those wishing to establish a business in Spain are free to do so.

14
Hibernation Rather Than Emigration

There are many who, for family or financial or other reasons would wish to spend only part of their retirement abroad each year. They are attracted to the pleasant economical way of life in a relatively warm and sunny climate, but would prefer not to cut the ties with the UK which the purchase of a foreign property and a move to it for year-round residence might entail. For them there is nowadays a ready solution. In the past few years a number of travel firms have started offering package tours of durations up to, in some cases, the whole of the cold British winter months, in 3- or 4-star hotels or in self-catering apartments in a number of the popular summer resort areas, at greatly reduced prices. These enable purchasers to spend all or most of the winter away from the rain and cold, without heating bills and in pleasant surroundings.

It is essential, however, before booking such a tour to ensure that it does not contain any proviso for considerable extra charges over the Christmas and New Year holiday periods.

Those wishing to spend the festive season at home with their families usually book one tour from, say, November to just before Christmas and then another which would commence in early January. This is a way of ensuring an enjoyable winter and an early spring sun-tan and also allows those thinking of eventual full-time residence in Spain to sample the way of life, and explore and select the site and type of accommodation that would suit them best.

Glossary of Spanish Terms

Abogado	A lawyer, solicitor
Alimentación	A supermarket
Al portador	The bearer
Aparejador	A professional who manages building sites
Apartado de Correos	A P.O. box.
Asesor fiscal	A financial consultant
Atico	The top storey of a building
Ayuntamiento	The town council
Bacalao	Salt cod
Bombona	A heavy-duty butane gas cylinder
Buzón	A pillar box
Cambio de Residencia	Change of residence
Campesino	A farm worker
Certificado de habitabilidad	A certificate that a building is ready for occupation (necessary before electricity can be connected).
Ciudad	A city
Cocina	A kitchen
Colegio	A college; a professional association
Comestibles	Groceries
Compañía de Electricidad	A local electricity company
Compañía Telefónica Nacional de España	The Spanish National Telephone Company
Con gas	Aerated mineral water
Contribución urbana	The equivalent of British rates
Copia simple	A legalised photocopy
Cortijo	Farm house
Coto privado	A private estate
Delegación de Hacienda	The tax collector's office
Dentista	A dentist
Dormitorio	A bedroom
En efectivo	In cash
Escritura	A deed
Estanco	A shop selling blank official forms and tobacco products
Farmacia	A chemist's shop

Glossary of Spanish Terms

Fiesta	A Spanish festival
Finca	House, land, farm, estate, factory (used widely)
Gasolina	92 octane petrol
Gestor	A professional who can negotiate on your behalf with Government departments
Gestoría	The office of a *gestor*
Guardia Civil	A para-military policeman
Guía	A guide book
Guía Telefónica	A telephone directory
Hogar de pensionistas	Pensioners' club
Huerto	An orchard
ICONA	The National Institute for the Conservation of Nature
Impuesto de transmisiones	A tax imposed when a property changes hands
Impuesto sobre el Patrimonio	Wealth tax
Impuesto sobre el Valor Añadido (IVA)	VAT
Instituto Nacional de la Seguridad	The National Social Security Institute
Internacional	International (telephone calls)
Interurbano	To Spanish towns (telephone calls)
Inyeccionista	A nurse specialising in giving injections
Jardín	A garden
Jardinero	A gardener
Letra	A post-dated promissory note
Lista de Correos	Mail delivery at Post Office (poste restante)
Mapa	A map
Médico	A doctor
Memoria	The specifications of a building drawn up by an architect
Menu turistico	Tourist menu
Ministerio	A ministry of government
Ministerio de Sanidad y Consumo	The Ministry of Health
Ministro	A government minister
Normal	92 octane petrol
Notario	A public notary charged with legalising documents
Obra nueva	A new construction
Obrero	A workman
Oficina de Correos	A post office
Parador	Hotel
Paso	A unit of telephone charge

Patrimonio	Patrimony
Piscina	A swimming pool
Plus valía	Municipal tax collected after property sale
Población	A town
Policía Rural	Police who patrol country areas
Polígono	A word often used for a development
Practicante	A nurse specialising in giving injections
Precio de Venta al Público (PVP)	Retail Price
Presidente	A chairman
Pueblo	A small village; a specialised urbanisation
Residencia	A residence permit
Seguro obligatorio	Third party insurance on a car
Sello de Correo	A postage stamp
Sin gas	Non-aerated mineral water
Su casa	Your house
Super	A supermarket; or 97 octane petrol
Supermercado	A supermarket
Talone	A cheque
Tapa	A lid or cover, snack
Tapas bars	Bars serving snacks
Testamento abierto	An 'open will'
Testamento cerrado	A 'closed will'
Tienda	A shop
Tráfico	A member of the traffic department of the Guardia Civil
Ultramarinos	Shop selling food
Urbanización	Urbanisation, development, housing estate
Venta ambulante	A travelling shop mounted in a van
Vivienda segundaria	A second home
Zarzuela	A Spanish operetta

Useful Addresses in the UK

Spanish Consulate General
20 Draycott Place,
London SW3 2RZ
Tel: 01 581 5921

Spanish Consulate General,
63 North Castle Street,
Edinburgh EH3.
Tel: 031 220 1843

Spanish Commercial Office,
22 Manchester Square,
London W1M 5AP
Tel: 01 486 0101

Spanish Chamber of Commerce,
5 Cavendish Square,
London W1M 0DP.
Tel: 01 637 9061

Spanish Consulate General,
1 Brooks House,
70 Spring Gardens,
Manchester 2.
Tel: 061 236 1233

Spanish Tourist Office,
57/58 St James's Street,
London SW1.
Tel: 01 499 0901/2/3

Spanish Institute (Cultural Activities),
102 Eaton Square,
London SW1.
Tel: 01 235 1484

LEGAL FIRMS PRACTISING IN SPANISH LAW

J. B. de Abando,
2 Wellington Square,
London SW3.
Tel: 01 730 7384

L. R. Barrero,
Amhurst Brown Martin &
Nicholson,
2 Duke Street,
St James's,
London SW1.
Tel: 01 930 2366

Colombotti and Partners,
1 Knightrider Street,
London EC4V 5JP.
Tel: 01 236 1514

M. Florez Valcarcel,
Notary Public,
21 Borough High Street,
London SE1 1XU.
Tel: 01 407 2141/407 1714

J. M. de Lorenzo,
63 Addison Road,
London E11.
Tel: 01 583 6995

Jose Medio,
40/41 Old Bond Street,
London W1X 3AF.
Tel: 01 409 2355/409 3152

Louis de Pinna,
5 Homer Row,
London W1H 1HU.
Tel: 01 724 3530

Fernando Scornik Gerstein,
32 St James's Street,
London SW1A 1HD.
Tel: 01 839 1581

Further names and addresses may be obtained from the
Law Society,
113 Chancery Lane,
London WC2.
Tel: 01 242 1222

Index

Absence from property 94
Accommodation 80
American newspapers 91
Anglican clergy 89
Annual charges 30
Art 88
Average temperatures 7–8

Bank certificates 41, 42
Banking in Spain 45–51
Bar-restaurants 81
BBC World Service 91
Beaches 86
Big game hunting 84
Books 92
Bookstalls 92
British banks in Spain 48–49
Bus services 74
Buying land and building 21
    fifteen important steps 21–24
Buying pre-owned villas and
    apartments 25–26

Car services 76
Cars 76
Charge and credit cards 48
Chemists 66
Church services 89–90
Cinema 87
Climate 5–6
Clothes, summer and winter
Commercial radio 90
Contemporary art 89
Co-ownership 35
Cuisine 69
Cultural life 87–93
Cruises 80

Diet 69
Domicile 4–5
Double taxation 62
Driving licence 76

English-language newspapers 92
English-language radio programmes
    from abroad 91
Escrituras 59
Exhibitions 89

Fiestas 80, 88
Fishing 85
Flamenco 87
Fruit 72
Funds transfer 47

Gestoria 37
Getting to Spain 6, 9
Gibraltar radio and TV 90
Glossary of Spanish terms 98–101
Golf clubs 82–83
Greetings 64
Guidebooks 92

Health care 66
Hibernation 97
Hotels 80
Household help 72

Importing
    effects 58–60
    pets 61
    private cars 60–61
Income tax 62
Inheritance tax 64
Inland transportation 74
    air 74
    bus 74
    car 75
    railway 74
    taxi 75
Insurance 66
Investment
    outside Spain by residents 64
    in Spanish companies 65

Index

IVA (VAT) 63

Language schools 93
Lending libraries 92
Local English-language publications 92

Magazines 90
Medical insurance 66
Modern art 88
Moroccan TV 90
Mortgages 40
Motoring 76–78
Museums 88
Music festivals 88

National Archaeological Museum 88
Newspapers 91
Notario (public notary) 37

On the beach 86

Paying for your property 41–44
Payment of bills whilst away 95
Pensioners' clubs 81–82
Petrol 78
Plus valía 64
Principal retirement areas
   Balearic Islands 14
   Canary Islands 15–16
   Costa de Almería 13
   Costa del Azahar 12
   Costa Blanca 12
   Costa Brava 10–11
   Costa Cálida 12
   Costa Dorada 11
   Costa de La Luz 14
   Costa del Sol 13–14
Property care during your absence 95
Property insurance 94
Public services and utilities 52–57
   electricity 54
   gas 54–55
   mail 56–57
   rubbish collection 56
   telegrams and cables 54
   telephones, private and public 52–53
   water 55–56

Radio relay programmes 90
Radio service 91
Religious services 89
Renting before buying 19–20
Restaurants 80
Road tax 76

Sailing 85
Satellite television 90
Security 31
Selecting a property 20
Shooting 84
Shopping 70–72
Small game hunting 84
Social customs 69–70
Social life 68–70
Spanish banks in UK 47
Spanish law practices in UK 102–103
Sports programmes on TV 90
Stage payments 42
SUR 89

Taxis 75
Television sets 90
Television (world-wide) 90–91
Tennis 85–86
Theatre 87
Time-sharing 34–35
Touring 78
Transfer tax 63
Typical deed 40–41

VAT (IVA) 63
Voice of America radio 91

UK daily newspapers 91
Useful addresses in UK 101

Visa requirements 17–18

Wardrobe 69
Wealth tax 63
Wills 65
Winter packages 97
Wireless 90
Working in Spain 96